# PRAYING LIKE CRAZY FOR YOUR KIDS

**Other books by Tamyra Horst**

*The Gift of Friendship*

*How to Hug a Heart*

*Ratty Bathrobes, Cranky Kids, and Other Romantic Moments*

*Time for All That's Important*

*A Woman of Worth*

TAMYRA HORST

# PRAYING LIKE CRAZY FOR YOUR KIDS

Pacific Press® Publishing Association
Nampa, Idaho
Oshawa, Ontario, Canada
www.pacificpress.com

Cover designed by Gerald Lee Monks

Cover design resources from Dreamstime.com

Inside design by Aaron Troia





Some names and details have been changed to protect identities.

Additional copies of this book are available by calling toll-free 1-800-765-6955 or visiting http://www.adventistbookcenter.com.

ISBN 13: 978-0-8163-2345-6

ISBN 10: 0-8163-2345-3

09 10 11 12 13 • 5 4 3 2 1

# Dedicated to

Joshua and Zachary,

for whom I have prayed like crazy

and always will.

You can count on it!

# Acknowledgments

To Miles Yoder, principal of Lancaster Mennonite School, who invited me to give a seminar to parents at a parent-teacher fellowship meeting. That invitation was the beginning of this book.

To Linda McCabe and Denise Reinwald, who not only supported me with prayer and encouragement as I wrote, but who also brainstormed ideas for the journaling section of each chapter.

To an amazing group of women who prayed for this project while I wrote: Starla, Tina, Lilly, Tracy, Linda, Denise, Tanya, Kathleen, and Judy.

# Contents

# Introduction

Dear Friend:

You've probably picked up this book because you have a burden to pray for your children. You may want to learn new ways to pray for them or may be looking for encouragement that prayer makes a difference. I hope you'll find both within these pages.

At the end of each chapter, I've included a few questions to help you apply what you've just read, and offered an opportunity to write down things and people you want to pray for in relationship to the chapter. This journaling opportunity is optional and included to enhance what you're reading. Know that what you discover in these pages is my prayer journey for my sons. It's not the only way to pray or the only things to pray about. When it comes to prayer, there really isn't a right or wrong way. There is no magic formula that if you follow all your prayers will be answered the way you desire. You don't have to convince God to move on behalf of your child or grandchild. God wants to and is working in their lives. He loves them more than you possibly can. Prayer is important often because of the work it does in us. It is honest conversation between an earthly parent and a heavenly Father. It has to be honest more than anything else. God wants it to be a conversation—intimate and personal. When you open your heart honestly before God about anything, and especially about your children, He hears and moves.

I've also included a "Pray for" section that recounts the main thoughts suggested to pray about in the chapter.

This book has been designed as a book for parents to pick up and read and deepen their own prayer journey for their children. However, it could also be used in a small group or book club. The journal thoughts at the end of each

chapter can be used as a catalyst for discussion and lead into a prayer time.

My prayers have been with you as I've written this book, and they continue to be with you as you pick it up and read it. I pray that God will help you find encouragement, resources, and tools, but, most of all, that you will discover an amazing Father who is working in your children's lives in ways you may not even know.

With love,

Tamyra Horst

# The Importance of Praying for Your Kids

*Be anxious for nothing [not even your kids], but in everything [including parenting] by prayer and supplication, with thanksgiving, let your requests be made known to God; and the peace of God, which surpasses all understanding, will guard your hearts and minds through Christ Jesus. —Philippians 4:6, 7*

Like most moms, I'll never forget the moment each of my sons was born.

My oldest came in the middle of a stormy night. My water broke, and the doctor encouraged us to come to the hospital. Labor began when we got there and lasted only an hour, but was incredibly intense. The umbilical cord was wrapped around my son's neck, and he was blue. My first words upon seeing him revealed my amazement at the miracle that I had just participated in: "It's a baby!"

Parenting has been one of the most amazing and most difficult adventures of my life.

I adored him from that moment on. Today he's a young adult forging his own life, but his smile still melts my heart every time I see it. And those black eyes with their twinkle—they always make me smile. There were moments when I thought I could never love another child as much as I loved him.

Three years later, in the middle of the day, his brother was

born. He was two weeks overdue, and this time labor lasted four hours. That doesn't sound long compared to other labor stories, but this baby seemed determined not to arrive no matter how hard I pushed. Then finally there he was—all eight pounds and seven ounces of him. They held him up for me to see; his eyes were wide open— and so was his mouth! I was totally consumed by love for him in that second. (Though I should've known what kind of child he would be by his stubbornness to be born and those wide-open eyes and open mouth!) He has brought me such joy and laughter.

My sons have always been one of the most important things in my life. I chose to quit my job and stay home with them. When they were in high school and I needed to go back to work to help financially with their Christian school tuition, I chose a part-time job that allowed me to work while they were in school, so I was home when they were. For years, I drove them to and from school because busses weren't available. I cheered at every cross-country meet in high school, volunteered at their schools, read hundreds of books to them, built Lego forts, learned to Rollerblade with them, climbed mountains with them, enjoyed camping in a tent because of them, learned to identify makes of cars because of my youngest son's passion for cars, and searched for books on backpacking through Europe when my oldest decided to go on the adventure of his life. I have chosen to make them a priority over career, material goods, and other things; and I have no regrets. Parenting has been one of the most amazing and most difficult adventures of my life.

I knew it would be.

My husband and I attended birthing classes before the birth of our first child. They taught us breathing techniques, what to expect, what to take to the hospital with us, and ways to cope with the hours of labor. The films they showed of women in labor frightened just about everyone in the class. But not me. I knew most women live

through labor. It would be hard. I'd have a story to tell when women talk. But I would most likely get through it one way or another. My fear was what came after delivery, when they handed me a tiny bundle and sent me home. Being totally responsible for this helpless baby frightened me terribly. I had no experience with babies. I was unsure of my parenting skills. Would I know what to do? What if he got hurt? Would I teach him all the right things? Would I make too many mistakes and scar him for life? Would he hate me? Love me? Be embarrassed by me?

The older they get, the more I find myself on my knees—both literally and figuratively.

While my husband was excited about having a baby in the house, I was more frightened and unsure about parenting than I had been about anything else in my life. So I did the one thing I knew how to do.

I began praying like crazy.

And I've never stopped.

In fact, the older they get, the more I find myself on my knees—both literally and figuratively. I have begged God, cried to God, gone to Him when my heart was in such pain for my children that I couldn't even form words or clear thoughts, I've praised Him, thanked Him, asked Him if He was sure He knew what He was doing, and constantly laid my sons at His feet and watched Him answer and move and work in their lives—not always the way I wanted, but always working the way He knew was best. And I've learned, and am continuing to learn, to trust Him with knowing what's best.

## Pray like crazy

While the Bible doesn't give specific instructions about

praying for our children, it does tell us to pray. About everything. *Everything* includes our children.

"Be anxious for nothing, but in everything by prayer and supplication, with thanksgiving, let your requests be made known to God; and the peace of God, which surpasses all understanding, will guard your hearts and minds through Christ Jesus" (Philippians 4:6, 7).

This verse teaches me to "be anxious for nothing," not even my children. Or my parenting. How?

"By prayer and supplication." By praying, giving it to God, and through supplication. *Supplication* means "humble, earnest prayer"; *earnest* means "serious." To earnestly pray means to pray with a seriousness and dedication that shows the depth of importance the request has to us. Basically, the Bible instructs us to pray like crazy and really mean it.

## That's not all

It's easy to stop there. But the scripture gives an important treasure that can be easy to overlook, but makes a huge difference in our prayers. "With thanksgiving . . ." To pray with thanksgiving. Sounds easy. But all too often, we forget to give thanks. We're so caught up in what we want God to do that we forget to thank Him. Or the things we're praying about are so painful and hard that we don't see what there is to be thankful for. Cancer. Rebellion. Walking away from God. A life-impacting or life-ending accident. Parents face so many things that cause us to wonder what we can find in them to give thanks for. While we'll talk about this in-depth in a later chapter, thanksgiving is huge in prayer because it reminds us of who God is and what He has done and can do. I've

We're so caught up in what we want God to do that we forget to thank Him.

found that no matter how difficult the challenge I am praying for concerning my sons, I can always thank God that He loves them even more than I do. I can thank Him that He knows what's best for them and is capable of moving in ways that I can't. I can thank Him for seeing the big picture and knowing what it takes now to get them where they need to be later. I can thank Him that He will allow only what's best for my sons' eternal purposes and nothing just for pain or harm to them. When I thank Him for these things, it gives me courage and strength, hope and peace.

## Prayer brings peace

In fact, verse 7 of Philippians 4 promises peace: "The peace of God, which surpasses all understanding, will guard your hearts and minds through Christ Jesus." God's peace. A peace that comes even when the world looks like a very nonpeaceful place.

We find . . . peace when we remember what kind of God we serve.

A peace that will "guard" our hearts and minds. A peace that will protect us from doubts, fears, and worry. From feelings of failure and worthlessness. Of despair and discouragement. We find this kind of peace when we remember what kind of God we serve and have trusted our kids to.

As parents, we can't fix every problem our kids face (nor should we). And not every hurt can be made better with a kiss and a Band-Aid. At some point, our children reach an age at which we can't make them do what we want them to, but have to trust that God is working in them to help them make the right choices. We have to choose the battles we fight with them, but we can take *everything* to God in prayer. Big or little, He cares—and is able to do way more than we're capable of.

So join me on a journey to learn how we can pray like crazy for our kids.

## Journal

- Remember when your children were born. Write a bit about their births, what you felt, what you feared, and what you were excited about.
- What has been the biggest prayer burden on your heart for your children?
- What can you be thankful for as you've prayed?
- What impressed you the most in this chapter?
- How will you apply the information from this chapter to your prayer life?
- Choose a scripture passage, personalize it by putting your name in it, and pray it for yourself as you begin or continue this journey of praying like crazy for your children. John 14:26, 27; Philippians 4:6, 7; 1 John 5:14, 15.
- Keep a record of other scripture passages you want to personalize and claim.

# Praying With Your Kids

*"You shall teach them to your children, speaking of them when you sit in your house, when you walk by the way, when you lie down, and when you rise up." —Deuteronomy 11:19*

We often ask people to pray for us. Or we tell people that we're praying for them. That's good. But there's something special about *hearing* someone pray for you. Hearing them pray specifically for the things that are important to you. Hearing them thank God for you. It gives you a glimpse of their heart toward you. It strengthens you. Even if nothing else has changed, just knowing that someone else is helping to carry your burden can give you courage.

That's true for our kids too.

When they hear us pray for them, it assures them that someone is on their side. That someone cares about the things that matter to them. That someone loves them.

And it teaches them to pray, what prayer sounds like, what to pray for, and how to pray for someone else. It makes praying for and with others a natural part of life. Something that they've always known.

In Deuteronomy 11:19, God admonishes parents to teach their children the principles and commandments of God, how to live " 'when you sit in your house, when you walk by the way, when you lie down, and when you rise up.' " These guidelines apply to praying with your children too.

## "When you sit in your house"

When are you sitting in your house?

*Meal times.* Meals are a natural time to pray. Often we limit that prayer time to just praying for the meal. "Bless this food to our bodies." But we can make it more than that. The family is gathered around the breakfast table. The day is just beginning. Ask, "What's going to be happening in your life today that we can be praying for?" At the end of the day and the family is sitting down for dinner, ask, "What can we pray for? What happened today? What were your challenges?" At the same time, we can look for things to thank God for. "What were the cool things that happened today? What can we thank God for?"

> When they hear us pray for them, it assures them that someone is on their side. That someone cares about the things that matter to them. That someone loves them.

In today's busy world, more and more families no longer sit down to dinner or breakfast or any other meal together. Make a commitment to have at least one meal each day together as a family. Use that family time as an opportunity not just to eat together, but to talk, catch up, and pray together.

*Computer time.* Many of us find ourselves sitting in our homes at the computer—some of us every day. E-mails are a new and great way of keeping in touch with people, including our kids. When our kids are away at school or have moved out on their own, we can pray with them through e-mail. We can type out a prayer for them in an e-mail and send it to them. It may not be the same thing as hearing someone pray, but imagine the smile that it can bring to their faces as they open an e-mail and read a prayer for

them. I can picture my son Josh, who currently lives four hours away, smiling and shaking his head a bit at his mom who prays via e-mail, but I can also imagine that it would be a blessing and be a reminder that no matter where he is, his mom is praying and caring—giving him evidence of it in more than just "I'm praying for you" written at the end of a note or e-mail or said at the end of a phone call.

We can pray with our children over the phone, by writing a prayer in a card and mailing it, or even by texting a short prayer. Maybe you know that your child is worried about a test at school or a presentation at work. A short text, "God, bless Kayla on this test," sent just as they're heading into class or the board room, can lighten that moment, giving them a shot of courage.

*Family worship.* When the boys were younger and both at home, we attempted to have family worship every day or at least on Friday evening—our "family night." We'd sing, read a Bible story or devotional, and pray together. Each person shared prayer requests. Sometimes my husband, Tim, or I would pray. Often we'd each pray. Sometimes we'd pray for the person next to us. Sometimes we'd simply mention a couple of the prayer requests for each person, making sure each person was covered.

Now that our boys are grown, we rarely have family worship together. Recently, Tim, Zach, and I had the opportunity to have family worship with Tim's youngest brother's family. They have a one-year-old and a two-year-old. We sang "Deep and Wide" and "This Little Light of Mine" and read Bible stories. It was fun, and I loved seeing my twenty-year-old son singing the songs we sang when he was little. And I pray that someday when he has a family of his own, it will be important to him to lead them in family worship.

## "When you walk by the way"

When this verse was written, most people walked from place to place. Today we walk, bike, drive, carpool, and

take mass transit. How do we pray with our children while we're getting somewhere?

I drove my sons back and forth to school until Josh got his driver's license. Twenty minutes each direction. Morning and afternoon. It took two hours of my day, but I never minded. (Well, maybe on really cold, snowy mornings.) It was time with my guys when we could talk without distractions.

As we'd drive to school in the morning, we'd talk about the day ahead—tests, homework, friends, things that would happen during the day, teachers they were struggling with. And just before we'd arrive at school, I would pray out loud for them. I wanted them to start their day knowing that mom was praying for anything and everything that mattered to them that day.

Occasionally, we would see accidents along the way. I'd immediately pray for those involved and the families getting the news that a loved one was hurt. Aloud. So my sons could hear. I knew it would be an example for them of praying for the things they saw around them, even for strangers.

One school year, I prayed for a family whose home we passed each day. I typically prayed silently for the young mom in the home whenever I drove by her house—and any time God reminded me of her. My sons knew I was praying for her. She had attended our church for a while and then stopped coming. She had made a few bad choices in her life. One morning, I felt compelled to pray for her aloud while the guys were in the car. "Lord, I've been praying that You will give her the desire to come back to church. Now please

I wanted them to start their day knowing that mom was praying for anything and everything that mattered to them that day.

give me the courage to stop and knock on her door and invite her back or cause me to run into her. Amen."

That very afternoon, I picked Josh up at school, and we headed to the local Wal-Mart while his brother stayed after school for cross-country practice. Josh headed for the electronics and music section while I picked up a few needed things. A few minutes later, Josh found me. Excited, he said, "Mom, she's here. You're going to run into her in the next aisle!"

> My simple prayer, prayed aloud in the car for my sons to hear, turned into an amazing story of how God immediately responded and worked a miracle. My sons witnessed the power of God and the power of prayer.

Josh had heard my prayer that morning. He knew that I had asked God to cause me to run into this woman. And there she was. He had seen her first. With Josh by my side, I turned the corner and "accidentally" bumped into this family I had been praying for. Mustering my courage, and knowing my son had heard my prayer and was watching, I went up to the young woman and said Hello. After chatting a bit, I said, "We've missed you at church."

"I've been wanting to come back," she replied. "But I wasn't sure if I'd be accepted after everything I've done."

I hugged her and assured her that we loved her and missed her. I was honest. My son was listening. "There may be people who might not be nice, but they will be few. Most of us just want to have you back."

That weekend my son found me as I was helping organize things for the worship service. "They're here, Mom!"

My simple prayer, prayed aloud in the car for my sons to hear, turned into an amazing story of how God immediately

responded and worked a miracle. My sons witnessed the power of God and the power of prayer.

## "When you lie down, and when you rise up"

My sons might be embarrassed if I told how old they were when I finally stopped "tucking them in" at night. It was one of the hardest transitions of parenting in my life. When Josh said, "Mom, I'm getting older. This is the last night for you to tuck me in," I thought my heart would break. I loved that time! I didn't see it as "tucking in" but as a special part of the day during which we talked and prayed and shared.

From the time they were little, I'd sit and talk with them for a few minutes before praying with them, kissing them, and turning off the light. We'd talk about their day, the things that concerned them, the things they enjoyed, their friends, what was going on in their friends' lives, problems at school, frustrations, and things they wanted to do. They'd ask random questions they were thinking about. Before leaving their room, I'd pray for them and all the things they talked about. Just us. One on one. Precious time. Of course, the things we talked about changed as they grew older. Our conversations often went deeper. Important talk. We'd talk about decisions, classes they'd take, about friends who were choosing to drink or smoke, the future, and girls, and then I'd pray about all we had talked about.

*Waiting up.* After Josh decided he was too old for mom to "tuck him in" at night, I still wanted to find that way to connect with Josh, hear about his day, and know what to pray for. So I started waiting up for him. I'd use those quiet nights to read and spend time with God.

When we built the upstairs to our home, my husband created a space in the hall between the boys' bedrooms that was large enough for a comfortable chair, small table,

and lamp. He said it could be my "worship chair." A place I could spend time with God and pray for my sons as I sat by their doors. That's where I'd wait for Josh.

He'd come home after being out with his friends and stretch his tall 6′ 2″ body on the floor and talk about his evening, his friends, and the things on his heart. I mostly listened. Occasionally I asked questions. While I no longer prayed aloud for him, I told him I'd be praying or that I was already praying for the things he was talking about.

One night as he lay stretched out on the floor, he asked, "So have I told you about what's going on in Craig's life?"

Craig was a friend of Josh's I was praying for. I had told Josh that I was praying. And he had shared some choices Craig was making that concerned him. Craig knew his friends didn't like what he was doing.

"No, what's going on?"

"He's decided to stop all that stuff. He's recommitted his life to God and is planning on going on a short-term mission trip this summer."

"Wow. I was praying for him."

"Yeah, I know. That's why I wanted to tell you."

This simple exchange encouraged me that Josh saw God working as a result of prayer; that there was a connection between what was happening in Craig's life now and Mom's prayers for this friend.

Even now that Josh is living in another state, and even though I haven't met many of his friends, he knows I'm praying. He tells me about his friends, and I ask about them by name. I ask specifically about the things that he's told me are going on in their lives. I remind him that I am praying for them.

More important, I remind him that I'm praying for him. For the things in his life that are important to him. I tell him when we're on the phone, in cards I send him, and at

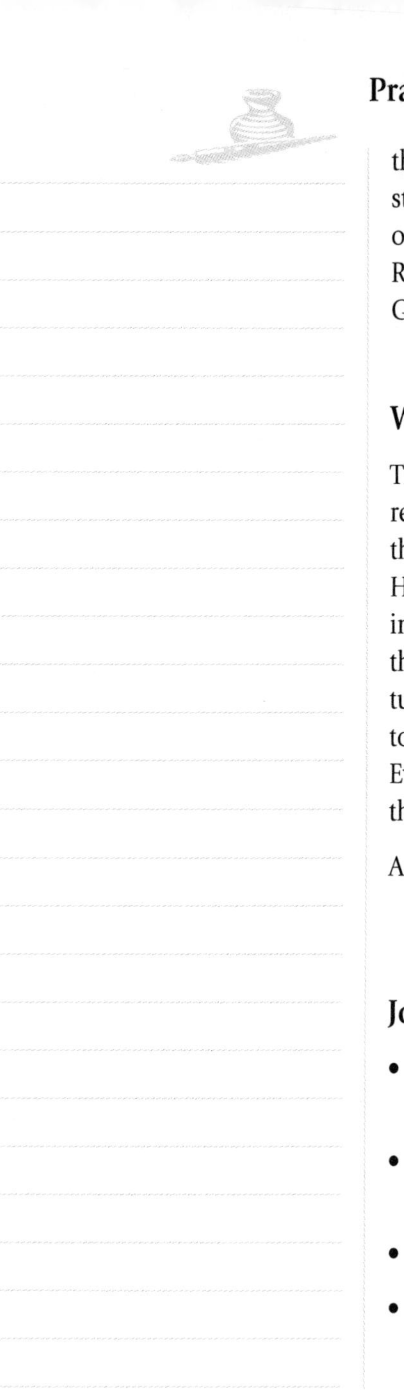

the end of e-mails. And whenever I get the opportunity, I still pray aloud for my sons, with them, though those opportunities can be harder to find as they grow older. Regardless of their age or busyness or distance, we can ask God for those times and intentionally look for them.

## When you can't pray with them

There may be times in their lives when our children aren't receptive to our praying with them. They may be going through a time when they're rejecting God, not wanting Him to be a part of their lives, and not seeing the power or importance of prayer. Yet we never have to stop praying *for* them on a daily basis. Every time we think about them, turning those thoughts into prayers. Every time we begin to worry about them, turning those worries into prayers. Every time the thought of them makes us smile, turning those smiles into thanksgiving to God.

And every chance we get, praying with them.

## Journaling

- When have been the times that your family has come together and prayed together?
- Remember a time when God blessed you significantly as you prayed together with your children.
- As you've read this chapter, what impressed you?
- What will you do as a result of reading this chapter? How will you pray with your children?
- Claim and personalize a scripture passage for yourself as you commit to praying together with your children: Deuteronomy 11:19; Matthew 18:19, 20.
- Keep a record of other Bible verses you want to personalize and claim.

# Praying Continuously

*Pray without ceasing.—1 Thessalonians 5:17*

I've worked with churches for many years. I've helped with a lot of different programs and processes designed to help churches assess where they are and then grow. One of those was Natural Church Development, a process that helps a church identify where it stands in eight characteristics that are a part of every church. In order to get that information, thirty church leaders and active members fill out a survey. Part of my job was to compile the data from that survey. One of the questions on the survey asked about prayer: How much time do you spend in prayer? Sadly, the majority of these church leaders and active members checked that they spend less than twenty minutes a day in prayer, and about half of those reported that they spend less than ten minutes a day in prayer.

The Bible tells us to pray without ceasing. "Without ceasing"—that means nonstop. All the time. All day long. Without stopping.

As a mom who is passionate about praying like crazy for my kids, I can't imagine spending only ten to twenty minutes a day praying. I feel like I need more time than that to pray just for my sons! There are moments when the burdens for my children alone fill my thoughts day and night. And then there are all the other things and people I want to pray for.

But praying without ceasing can seem like an incredibly daunting task. How do we pray without ceasing for our children?

## The position of prayer

First, its important to note that prayer doesn't have to mean being on your knees with your eyes closed. You can pray standing up, sitting down, lying in bed, walking, or running. The position doesn't matter. And your eyes can be opened or closed. (If you're praying when you're moving or driving, they better be open!) You can pray silently or aloud; you can write your prayers. (I love journaling prayers!) You can pray by yourself or in a group. Prayers can be long or short, just a sentence. I've had prayers that are only "God, please!" Prayer is a conversation between an individual and God. They can be about one thing specifically or a lot of things randomly. (Conversation with me can often be very random, so my prayers can flit from topic to topic. Fortunately, God can follow my thinking.) The words of a song may form our prayers—singing the song as a prayer to God.

Prayer doesn't have to mean being on your knees with your eyes closed. You can pray standing up, sitting down, lying in bed, walking, or running. The position doesn't matter. And your eyes can be opened or closed.

Sometimes we may not even be able to form the words to pray. God knows this too. "We do not know what we should pray for as we ought, but the Spirit Himself makes intercession for us with groanings which cannot be uttered" (Romans 8:26). In those moments, we can cry out to God, "Oh, God!" and the Spirit Himself will pray for us with words we don't even know to say.

So knowing that prayer can take a lot of different forms and can happen in any circumstance or place, how can we pray without ceasing for our children?

## Life prompts

We can allow life to prompt our prayers.

When we're doing the laundry and are folding our kids' clothes, pray for them.

When we're cleaning their room or making their beds (of course, this is when they're little, because as they grow older, this will be their responsibility!), we can pray for them.

When we're walking through the house and see a picture of them, or perhaps we have their picture in our office, let that picture be a reminder to pray.

As we're cooking dinner or packing their lunch, pray for them.

## While driving

I often pray when I'm driving. I have a fifty-minute commute each way to work. Fifty minutes all by myself, when I can do little besides drive, sing, and pray. I often use that quiet time as an opportunity to talk to God, especially about my sons, usually talking aloud to God.

## Waiting up

Sometimes when I was waiting up for the boys to get home at night, I'd pray, usually journaling my prayers for them, or turning the scriptures I was reading into prayers for them.

## In the middle of the night

Typically, I try to stay awake when I'm praying. But when I wake up in the middle of the night and can't go back to sleep, I pray myself back to sleep, praying until I fall asleep again and turning those restless moments into conversations

with a God who never sleeps. I may ask God, "What do You want me to pray about right now?" but often I'll just pray for my sons, taking those concerns I have for them and praying silently until I fall asleep again.

## Thoughts and worries

When you find yourself thinking about your kids, especially when you're worrying, going over and over those things that are heavy on your heart for them, turn those thoughts and worries into prayers. Remember to thank God that He is able and will do mighty things and that He *is* doing mighty things in response to your prayers for your children. Pretty soon those worries and fears will fade into peace as you are reminded that God is in control.

When you find yourself thinking about your kids, especially when you're worrying, going over and over those things that are heavy on your heart for them, turn those thoughts and worries into prayers.

## Chunks of time

While I pray throughout the day for my children, using every prompt and opportunity to be reminded to take my concerns and thoughts to God, it is important to me to also take a chunk of time and pray in a focused way. My random, spontaneous prayers are important, and God answers and loves the flowing conversation throughout the day and night. However, that chunk of time where I'm praying for a period of time (I don't have a specific amount of time, though I love to make this time happen at the beginning of the day) enables me to pray regularly and with focus.

As I pray throughout the day, I may pray about whatever pops into my mind or specifically for the thing that weighs heaviest on my heart for my sons, but that scheduled prayer time is when I pray for their relationship with God, for God to bring godly Christian friends into their lives, for them to pursue God's purpose and passion for their lives, and for those things that are regular prayer requests for their lives—a reminder to me and to God what is most important to me for them.

Praying for our children at every opportunity is a reminder that He is always there, listening and caring and that we're not in this parenting thing alone.

## We're not alone

This constant focus on praying for our children at every opportunity is a reminder that He is always there, listening and caring and that we're not in this parenting thing alone. God is in control and can do amazing things on behalf of our kids—no matter how old or young they are.

## Journal

- How have you prayed continuously for your children? How has God blessed as a result?
- What impressed you in this chapter? How will you pray more continuously for your children?
- What have been the things you have worried about the most about your children?
- Write a prayer to God, giving Him these worries.
- How will you turn your worries into prayers?

## Praying Like Crazy for Your Kids

- What is the biggest challenge in praying for your children?
- Write a prayer giving the challenge to God and asking Him for a way around it.
- Have you ever felt alone in your parenting? Write a prayer to God telling Him about it and asking Him to help you lean on Him and know that He's walking with you in this journey.
- Claim a scripture passage, personalize it with your name, and pray for yourself as you pray continuously for your kids. Deuteronomy 31:6; Isaiah 41:10.
- Keep a record of other scripture passages you want to personalize and claim.

# Praying for Their Spiritual Lives

*For this reason I bow my knees to the Father of our Lord Jesus Christ, from whom the whole family in heaven and earth is named, that He would grant you, according to the riches of His glory, to be strengthened with might through His Spirit in the inner man, that Christ may dwell in your hearts through faith; that you, being rooted and grounded in love, may be able to comprehend with all the saints what is the width and length and depth and height—to know the love of Christ which passes [all] knowledge; that you may be filled with all the fullness of God.*
*—Ephesians 3:14–19*

One of the things that has been most important to me for my sons is their relationship with God. More than anything else, I want them to know God, to trust God, walk with God daily, and live passionately for Him, even if it's in a quiet way.

I've never wanted God and church to be merely a habit, something they did just as part of a routine. I want more for them. I want them to know God intimately—a personal, intimate relationship with a God they know loves them and delights in them.

I truly believe that there is a spiritual battle going on over our children. The devil doesn't want them to know God. And if he can't stop them from knowing God, then he'll

do all he can to make sure that what they know is wrong, that they'll believe that God is judgmental or critical or focused on rules. He'll get them to buy into the current thinking that God exists, but that He's no longer interested or involved in our lives. The devil will tempt them to be too busy, even with good things, or try to draw them into being so focused on obeying all the rules that they don't have time for or aren't focused on a relationship with God.

When he can, the devil will lure them away from God with work, money, sports, hobbies, obsession over appearance, drinking, drugs, and anything else that he can use. Some of it perfectly fine stuff; it's not just people who are living an openly rebellious life who don't have time for God. Our children can be successful in the world but not be successful in knowing God.

If the devil can't lure them away from church, he often uses the church to cause them to dislike God, making our young people see the church as a place full of rules, or of people who aren't loving and accepting but are judgmental and critical. He shows them people who look good sitting in the sanctuary but live differently during the week. Many in today's postmodern generation like God, but don't like the church.

Many in today's postmodern generation like God, but don't like the church.

As parents, we can teach and live as real Christians in front of our kids, but we can also pray specifically for their relationship with God, asking Him to make Himself known to our children in ways that they can understand.

## An intimate, real walk

Almost every day I pray that God will help my sons know Him in a real and personal way. Not just a habit or way of life, but as an intimate God who loves them, delights in

them, communicates with them, listens to them, and is interested in everything and anything on their hearts and minds.

I attempted to teach them how to have a personal relationship with God as they were growing up. We raised our sons in church and sent them to Christian schools. They went to Vacation Bible School each year and Christian summer camp. They became involved in church ministries. Their best friends went to the same church or school. We had small-group Bible studies in our home and attempted to have worship at home. I read books to them about how God had changed people's lives, about Christians who served God with their whole heart and lives. I prayed with them every day. My husband taught them about God through nature, instilling in them a love for mountains and the ocean and all of the outdoors.

In order to truly answer my prayers and His desire for my sons, God has taken them on a journey with a few twists and turns that hasn't always been easy or looked good.

When the boys were small, they loved going to church and loved Jesus. Both committed their lives to God and asked to be baptized at an early age. Josh loved to sing hymns in church; he even sang "Amazing Grace" for a community event. Zach served as the Community Services leader for our church when he was only ten years old. God was answering my prayers. This is what I wanted. It looked so good.

But God knew it needed to go deeper, that their walk with Him had to be about their relationship with Him. I had asked Him to not let it just be a way of life—a routine they learned from the time they were born and just did. So in

order to truly answer my prayers and His desire for my sons, God has taken them on a journey with a few twists and turns that hasn't always been easy or looked good.

God doesn't just zap spirituality into our kids. Praying for their spiritual lives doesn't mean that *poof!* they instantly become spiritual giants who never falter or question or doubt.

In fact, my older son has done just that. Question, wonder, and search. He's read books on various faiths. He's attended services of many denominations. He's watched videos attempting to disprove Christianity and has researched their claims afterward to find the truth.

At first, this questioning and seeking was scary to his dad and me. What if our son decided he didn't believe? What if he didn't keep the faith we had attempted to pass on to him?

As I've prayed and watched, I've recognized that this testing and seeking is good. It has given God numerous opportunities to show Josh truth and to reinforce what he's learned all his life. It is building *Josh's* faith, building *his* relationship with God, showing him not only how to seek out truth, but making that truth stronger in his thinking as he learns and studies and proves it.

I've wrestled with God over Josh's search. I've wondered why God couldn't just zap him, yet knowing that the seeking and questioning will help Josh become stronger. I've realized that I prayed God would make Josh's faith strong and real, but feared God wouldn't be big enough to stand up to Josh's questions. God is big enough. So I'm learning to trust, to praise and thank God for the seeking that is drawing Josh closer, and praising Him for being a God who wants that—who longs for my sons to truly know Him and be known by Him.

## Experience God

One of the ways God makes Himself known is by allowing

His children to experience Him, to catch a glimpse of His character, to sense His presence, to hear His words, and to recognize Him at work through them.

I pray that my sons will experience God daily, while at work, hanging out with friends, in the quiet of their day, or in the ways He uses them to impact other people. I pray that they will encounter and recognize God in such a way that it will make a radical impact on their lives. I know and believe God is at work in them and pray that they will recognize that it's He. Too many of us miss out on God, not because He's not there, but because we don't recognize Him. I long for God to open my sons' eyes to His work, not only in their own lives, but in the lives of people around them.

I often ask God to give my sons and their friends a deep hunger for Him, a desire to know Him more. During Josh's senior year in high school, his Bible teacher invited me to come share about our denomination and beliefs with both Josh's class and the other senior Bible class. It was a very interesting experience sharing, answering questions, and getting to know Josh's classmates. After class, one of his friends asked Josh more questions and asked if he thought I'd be willing to meet with her sometime to talk more. He knew I would be. He knew I prayed specifically for his friends, including for their spiritual walk. Not only did it give Josh the opportunity to put words to his own beliefs in conversation with a friend, but he saw the Holy Spirit at work in the life of a young woman who struggled with choices and with God. It reminded him that God is at work and interested. He experienced God.

I love it when one of my kids will tell me a story about how God showed up during the day. (As if He wasn't there all along!) They've told stories of friends with questions or friends who have given up drugs or alcohol. Josh shared how a friend was hanging out after school working on a project with a teacher who felt impressed to talk about his relationship with God (this was a Christian school) in

such a way that the friend surrendered his heart to God and tossed out the alcohol he had hidden at home. Josh was impressed by the changes in his friend's attitude and heart. He had been concerned about this friend for a while. The next night, his friend was killed in an accident. Josh saw that God loved his friend so much that He reached his heart before he lost his life. He experienced God's concern and timing.

I want my kids to experience many aspects of God—His might and power, His majesty and peace, His sense of humor, His grace and character, and His love.

## Comprehend God's love

One of the things that I have really wanted to convey to my sons is that God loves them. It sounds so simple and is so easy to say. "Yes, God loves me." We sing about it, talk about it, but it's not easy to live at the core of who we are, to truly believe that God loves us unconditionally all the time. If we don't truly believe His love, it is hard to really trust Him, to know that even when difficult and painful things happen, God is still there, still involved, still caring and working to redeem the pain. Too often, as prayers seemingly go unanswered and difficulties and pain become overwhelming, we forget God loves us and wonder where He is. We wonder whether He's forgotten us, and we no longer sense His presence or His peace.

> I want my sons to be so convinced of God's love for them that no matter what happens in their lives, they won't question God's love or presence, but will trust Him.

I want my sons to be so convinced of God's love for them that no matter what happens in their lives, they won't question God's love or presence, but will trust Him.

It's hard. I'm not living there myself many days.

But I continue to pray.

Sometimes I pray Paul's beautiful prayer in Ephesians 3:

> For this reason I bow my knees to the Father of our Lord Jesus Christ, from whom the whole family in heaven and earth is named, that He would grant you, according to the riches of His glory, to be strengthened with might through His Spirit in the inner man, that Christ may dwell in your hearts through faith; that you, being rooted and grounded in love, may be able to comprehend with all the saints what is the width and length and depth and height—to know the love of Christ which passes [all] knowledge; that you may be filled with all the fullness of God (verses 14–19).

What a beautiful prayer. In the margin of my Bible, I've written, "This is one of the most beautiful and powerful prayers! My favorite. I claim it for my guys."

Paul is praying for the Ephesians to be able to comprehend a little more of God's love. He begins his prayer, "For this reason." To know the reason, you have to read the previous verse. "Therefore I ask that you do not lose heart at my tribulations for you" (verse 13).

Paul knew that it was easy to lose heart when tribulations come to you or to those you love. He also knew how to not lose heart, and that's the reason he prayed that they would be "rooted and grounded in love" and would be able to comprehend "the width and length and depth and height—to know the love of Christ which passes [all] knowledge." He knew they would never totally grasp or understand God's love fully—it "passes [all] knowledge." But he knew

that as they began to comprehend it more and more and were rooted and grounded in it—as it became the foundation that they stood on, the core of who they were—they wouldn't lose heart when trials came.

So I pray Paul's prayer for my sons, knowing that the more they understand and live in God's love, the stronger they'll be when trials come and the more confident their daily lives will be.

Sometimes my prayers are simple. A tag at the end of a prayer or a short prayer lifted during the day, "God, remind my sons that You love them." I believe God delights in answering these prayers, in revealing His love to His beloved children.

> Thanking God for the fruit we see Him growing in our children's lives not only reminds us to be grateful, but helps us to see the fruit that is growing.

## Fruit of the Spirit

As our children grow in their relationship with God, they will grow themselves. He will work in them to grow them to spiritual maturity. This will be evident by the fruit of the Spirit in their lives.

"The fruit of the Spirit is love, joy, peace, longsuffering, kindness, goodness, faithfulness, gentleness, self-control" (Galatians 5:22, 23).

These characteristics emerge out of a growing relationship with God. As parents, we can pray that God grows these fruit in the lives of our children, making them loving, joyful, peaceful, patient, kind, good, faithful, gentle, and self-controlled. We can also ask God to deepen these qualities in them.

As important as it is to pray and ask, it's also important for

us to thank. I think that thanking God for the fruit we see Him growing in our children's lives not only reminds us to be grateful, but helps us to see the fruit that is growing. Some days, it's easy to focus on what our kids still lack. Our prayers often reflect this, as well, with a constant, urgent asking. And we should pray in this way. (This book is all about praying like crazy!) But to thank God for the fruit we see growing as evidence of their spiritual closeness with God, encourages us that God is at work and is answering our prayers, reminding us, too, that He loves our children deeply.

## God's favor

God does love our children. He longs to bless them and does so in answer to our prayers.

Jabez was a man who longed for God's blessing. He didn't want to live up to his name, which means "he will cause pain." (Parents sometimes give their kids names that are hard to live with, but this name is like a warning that would keep people away.) He didn't want to cause pain. He wanted blessing. So he asked God, "Oh, that You would bless me indeed."

It seems like such a bold prayer. "Bless me indeed" (much, greatly). "Enlarge my territory" (border). "Keep Your hand on me. Keep me from evil. Don't let me cause pain."

But the significant thing is that God answered affirmatively. *So* "God granted him what he requested" (see 1 Chronicles 4:9–11).

God likes bold prayers.

He likes doing things that are so big that they could be done only by God.

He loves blessing His kids.

I know I love giving gifts to my children. I like finding that one thing I know they'll enjoy and buying it for them,

especially for no reason. I enjoy the look on their faces, the joy they experience.

I inherited that from my Father, who can give much better gifts than I know how to give and who loves doing it more.

Sometimes He gives for no reason. Other times He waits to be asked. As parents, we can ask on behalf of our children, "God, bless my child indeed."

I don't believe that blessing means a golden life or a golden touch—that everything works out perfectly or that they're incredibly rich and have no problems. I do believe that God longs to bless them spiritually with eternal treasures and expand their influence for Him, that He longs to walk beside them daily with His hand constantly on them, through the good times and the bad, and that He longs to keep them from evil and from causing others pain. When I ask God to bless my sons indeed, I'm asking for a rich spiritual blessing that will last through eternity, not a temporary blessing of big houses, cars, and money in the bank (though because I all too often forget the blessings of tough times, I think I want God to give them enough that they're comfortable and not struggling).

The "blessing indeed" I ask Him for is an intimate, dynamic, personal, and growing relationship with a God they know loves them and can be trusted no matter what.

## Pray for:

1. them to know God in a real way, intimately and personally;
2. God to surround them with angels who will protect them from spiritual harm;
3. them to truly seek God, to have a desire for truth and an understanding of God;
4. them to have a hunger for more of God;

5. them to desire to know God more;
6. them to experience God's character, His grace, and His sense of humor;
7. them to be able to believe God loves them at their core and to be able to live life from this belief;
8. them to be able to trust God's love especially in the middle of pain and trials;
9. the fruit of the Spirit—love, joy, peace, longsuffering, kindness, goodness, faithfulness, gentleness, self-control—to grow in them;
10. and God to bless them indeed, enlarge their territory, keep His hand on them, and keep them from evil.

## Journal

- How have you seen God lead in your children's spiritual lives?
- Write a prayer thanking Him for how He has been leading.
- What areas of their spiritual walk do you want to pray for more specifically?
- Write a prayer to God for those things now.
- What influenced you most in this chapter?
- How will you commit to praying for your children's spiritual walk?
- Personalize and pray one of these scriptures for your children: 1 Corinthians 1:4–9; Ephesians 1:17–19; Ephesians 3:14–19; Ephesians 6:10–18. Write it out in prayer form here.
- Keep a record of other scriptures you want to personalize and claim.

# Praying for Their Relationships

Relationships are important to us. They add much to our lives—good things, fun, caring, support, and encouragement. They can also add tough things—conflict, drama, jealousy, competition, and pain.

People affect us, for good or for bad, helping us to grow stronger and more into the person God created us to be, or hindering our growth either by wounding us or by influencing us to make poor choices.

It's important to pray for the people who interact with our kids—for both good and bad—such as friends, peers, bosses, and coworkers.

## Praying for their friends

Friendships are important to kids, especially as they move into the teen years. Their friends will influence the things they do, the places they go, the music they listen to, the movies or television they watch, the clothes they wear, their attitudes toward parents, school, church, God, and the choices they make regarding drugs, alcohol, sex, and other life-impacting things.

As parents, we need to be praying specifically for their friendships.

One of the first things to pray for is the friends they choose. Even now that my children are grown, I continue to pray that God will bring godly Christian friends into their lives. It's a request I've been praying since they were small and first making friends. Back then, I had more control over their choices. Friends were usually children of

my friends, kids they went to church and school with. As our children grow older and especially as they move into college and careers, we may not even know all their friends. But we can still pray that God will guide them as they choose friends and build relationships.

> Friendships are important to kids, especially as they move into the teen years. Their friends will influence the things they do, . . . and the choices they make.

As they've made friends on their own, I pray for their friends by name, praying for specific things as I've heard my kids talk or as they've shared things with me. I listen to their conversations. I learn the names of their friends, even if I have never met them. I attempt to remember what I can about each one, as they share stories and life with me. I want to know their friends as well as I can so that I can pray even more specifically for them.

When my children share about their friends and the choices they're making, I attempt to not condemn or judge or put their friends down. When they've shared about friends who are drinking or smoking or having sex or trying drugs, I do talk to my sons about those things and remind them about the influence friends can have, but I also talk about how they can influence their friends for good. I don't put their friends down for the choices they're making. I know that if I do, my sons will close down communication. They're not going to share honestly with me about their friends if they think I'm going to respond with anger, judgment, or criticism. They'll share only if they know that I will respond with care and concern, still liking their friends, but sharing their concern for the choices they've made and praying about those choices.

It's a fine line. We know friends influence each other. We know that if kids are drinking, they may encourage their

other friends to join them. Or if one kid is doing something, others, including our own, may follow suit because they want to be cool and fit in. We don't want our kids getting involved in these things. But by the time our kids get to the age where friends are making these decisions, they should already know where we stand on these issues. Conversations about drinking, drugs, smoking, premarital sex, cheating, cutting school, bullying, cyber-bullying, etc., will have already happened enough that not only do they know what we believe, but we will have talked about our expectations for their behavior and talked about how they can respond when their friends ask them to try any of these things.

There are times when I have asked God to intervene and end dangerous friendships and to somehow take away the impact of a friend who is influencing my child in a negative way.

While I used these conversations with my sons as opportunities to remind them of right and wrong and how to respond, the focus was on caring about their friends and praying for them. I wanted them to talk to me about what was going on, so I was careful to keep the doors of communication open.

There are times when I have asked God to intervene and end dangerous friendships and to somehow take away the impact of a friend who is influencing my child in a negative way. Not long ago, I was concerned about the influence of one of their friends. So I took it to God. I shared my concerns about the friendship with God and asked Him to move that friend away if he was a problem. Within a month that friend chose to go to a different school and moved away. While he is still my son's friend, his influence is now much more limited.

## Praying for Their Relationships

My sons attended Christian schools. Their friends were all from Christian homes. They were active in their youth groups. They were good kids. But some of them still got in trouble—drinking, smoking, driving too fast, or having sex with their girlfriends.

But there were other things I prayed for, such as illness, bullies, girl-boy relationships, depression, discouragement, and schoolwork.

Sometimes I did more than pray.

When one of Josh's friends was struggling with college and contemplating dropping out his senior year, not only did I pray, but I sent this friend care packages filled with cookies and notes of encouragement.

There may be times when your child won't want you involved in the lives of their friends. . . . Pray anyway.

I talked to their friends when they came over.

I *oohed* and *aahed* over an engagement ring and talked about the nervousness of one friend as he made plans to talk to the girl's dad, all the while praying that God would give wisdom and guidance to a couple I thought was too young to be getting married.

We discussed career goals, and I prayed that God would show them His purpose and direction.

A friend of Josh's hiked with us one afternoon. She and I talked about a group she was a part of that mentored young girls. I shared about a resource I had put together for young women that tackled the topic of beauty—and then sent her a copy of it. (She told Josh that his family was very cool.)

A friend of Zach's was considering becoming a pastor. I work in ministry and had the opportunity to invite her to speak and lead out in seminars, giving her opportunities

while talking to her and praying for her as she explored working with young people.

There may be times when your child won't want you involved in the lives of their friends. They may be reluctant to talk to you about their friends or introduce you. Pray anyway. God knows who they are and what's happening.

## Pray for their peers

Not everyone their age will be a friend, but may influence them anyway. Their peers in the classroom or at work can still influence their lives.

*Pray for their classmates.* I often prayed for their entire school, especially that God will raise up kids who will be spiritual leaders (more on this topic in another chapter).

*Pray for the bullies in their lives.* When Zach was in middle school, a boy who had been a good friend of his in elementary school turned on him. He started pushing him around, both verbally and physically. He spread lies. He did it not only to Zach but to a number of other kids in their class. When parents got together, the mention of his name brought a response; all the parents knew of him. I prayed for him, that God would convict him, change him, and empower others to stand up to him.

## Pray for their coworkers and bosses

*Pray for their coworkers.* The people they work with—whether coworkers at McDonald's, where they work after school, or the person in the next cubicle as an adult, these are the people our kids spend a lot of time with. Pray for their influence. Pray that God will use your children to influence them.

*Pray for their bosses,* that they will see the potential in your children and help them to live up to it. I typically pray that God will bring my kids godly, Christian bosses. And if they're not Christian, I pray for the influence of my kids on them and for their salvation.

## Pray for God in the lives of their friends

No matter the age of my children and their friends, I pray that God will draw them closer. Whether they're already Christians or whether they don't have a relationship with God, I pray that God will give them a hunger for Him, a passion for Him, and that they will long to know truth. I ask God to show them His will for their lives and give them the drive to pursue that purpose.

I believe that part of my role as a parent is to know and pray for the friends that God brings into my sons' lives.

I pray that God will reveal more of Himself, more of His love for them. And that He will help them to discover and live the value He has given them.

I believe that part of my role as a parent is to know and pray for the friends that God brings into my sons' lives.

## Pray for:

1. God to bring godly Christian friends into their lives;
2. their friends and their specific needs and choices;
3. their friends to have a real and intimate relationship with God;
4. their friends to know God's plan for their lives and have the courage and confidence to pursue it;
5. their peers;
6. bullies in their lives to be convicted and changed;
7. coworkers to be a good influence;

8. and bosses to be godly people who will see their potential and help them to grow.

## Journal

- How have you seen God work in your children's lives through their friends—for good or bad?
- Who are their friends whom you are praying for or will commit to pray for?
- What are specific things you want to pray for in these friends' lives?
- Write a prayer for them.
- Are there peers who influence your children? Who are they? How can you, or will you, pray for them?
- Write a prayer for them.
- If your children have jobs, who are their bosses? Who are their coworkers?
- How can you, or will you, be praying for them?
- Write a prayer for them.
- Personalize and claim a scripture for your children: Ecclesiastes 4:9, 10; 1 Corinthians 1:10; 1 Thessalonians 5:11. Write it out as a prayer.
- Keep a record of other scriptures you want to personalize and claim.

# Praying for the Places They Learn

Our kids typically spend one hundred eighty days a year in school—that's about half the year—for thirteen years, counting kindergarten through high school, and seventeen years if four years of college are included. They'll spend more of their waking hours on a school day in a classroom than at home.

Whether their school is a public school or a private school, the schools our children attend need to be covered in prayer.

School is a huge part of their lives, not just in the amount of time spent there, but what they learn there, in the classroom and in the halls and cafeteria, will impact them forever.

Now add to that sports, church, youth groups, Sabbath School, and extracurricular activities at school, such as band, clubs, and committees.

School is an important focus for prayer.

## Pray for their school

Whether their school is a public school or a private school, the schools our children attend need to be covered in prayer. We can be praying for many things: their teachers, the administration, the school board, other students, the student leadership, the opportunities the school offers, the school's finances—especially if it's a private school that depends on tuition.

## Praying Like Crazy for Your Kids

I often prayed for the teachers to know God in a real and intimate way and that God would guide them and give them wisdom as they prepared for and taught their classes. Sometimes I would send handwritten notes to my sons' teachers at the beginning of the semester to let them know I was praying for them. It was amazing how often teachers would call or write back, telling me how important my prayer support was to them and how much it meant to them.

I also prayed that my sons' teachers would see their potential, that they would know how to reach them through their learning styles and interests, and that they would influence them for God.

Many of these teachers played important roles in my sons' lives. When each of the guys turned eighteen, we planned a special birthday party, inviting the godly men who had influenced their lives to come and talk to them about what it meant to live as a godly man and then to pray for them and their lives. Several of their teachers were among those who were invited to attend because of the role they played in their lives. They had become more than teachers who stood up front and taught a subject, but godly men who influenced them beyond the classroom.

My sons attended Christian school all the way through high school. But even though it was a Christian school and the teachers all had a commitment to Christ, some of the students didn't necessarily have that commitment. So I prayed that God would draw the students to Him and that God would bring a spiritual revival to the campus. I asked Him to raise up spiritual leaders among the students and that they would influence my sons. I prayed that my sons would be spiritual leaders in their schools.

Because I became involved in each of their schools, volunteering, helping in classrooms, and serving as the Parent-Teacher Fellowship president, I met other students. Some were friends of my sons, and some weren't. I prayed specifically for them. When I heard a story of a student

who had lost a parent or grandparent or who was battling an illness (and there were many of these stories throughout each school year!), I would pray for these students and their situations, even if I had never met them.

## Pray for the extras

Often when our children attend school, they're a part of lot of things that aren't directly related to the classroom, such as sports, music groups, clubs, and committees. We encouraged our sons to be involved in at least one extracurricular activity a year (but no more than one at a time because we didn't want them to be overcommitted). I prayed about their decisions—that God would guide them and help them to be where He could best reach them. More than once, one of the guys would consider joining something but not make the team or get the part, or he would eventually decide the activity wasn't for him. I trusted God to guide and that if one of them went out for something that wasn't good, God would prevent it. One year Josh tried out for the school play. He had been in numerous school plays before, usually getting the lead role. So we knew that drama was something he was good at. But when the roles were posted, he didn't get a part. Later I heard that the cast was pretty rowdy and had even spent a night skinny-dipping in the school pond. It reminded me that God did know the best places for my sons and was protecting and guiding them.

> I prayed about their decisions—that God would guide them and help them to be where He could best reach them.

Both boys joined their school's cross-country team. Tough sport! They ran 3.1 miles across fields and up and down hills at their meets. I prayed for their teammates. I prayed for their coaches. At meets, there were often kids who ran

too hard and got sick, or collapsed, or struggled at the end. I prayed for them. I prayed for my sons to do their best and to feel a part of their team.

One season, Zach set a goal to improve his time at each meet. Every time he ran, I cheered him on, not totally believing that he could run faster than the week before, but praying that God would give him strength (and help him with disappointment if he didn't!). He surprised us many weeks when we thought the course was just too hard to run faster than the week before, but he did. He knew I was praying and cheering him on. As he continued to meet his goal, others got in on the cheering and celebrating. At the awards banquet at the end of the season, Zach was recognized for beating his own record week after week. Some of his best memories of high school and feelings of accomplishment came from being a part of this team.

## Pray for the challenges they face

Some kids breeze through school without seeming to try.

I was one of those students. Good grades weren't hard and didn't require a lot of extra effort. My son Josh inherited my study habits. He did his work and got his assignments in on time. School wasn't tough for him. There was the occasional subject that required more and a moment or two in his education when he got a little sidetracked and needed to refocus and get back into it.

Zach was not like his brother or me. He didn't like doing homework and couldn't understand why he had to show his work if he could figure out the answer in his head. He often questioned why and procrastinated on projects. Report card after report card said the same thing, "Zach does great on tests but fails to hand in homework," or "Zach doesn't work up to potential."

He was an intelligent and capable kid who didn't always want to do the work. It was frustrating.

I prayed a lot. (And battled with him often.)

I prayed for wisdom about motivating him.

I prayed for his teachers—that they would see his potential and understand his learning style and work with it all to help him succeed.

I prayed that God would convict him and motivate him.

I prayed for God to guide and help him to learn.

School will offer different challenges to different kids based on their personalities, learning styles, and interests. As parents, we can recognize the specific challenges our children face and pray for them, whether it's a shy kid who finds the social aspect of school difficult, a sensitive child who is easily hurt by the words of mean kids, a student who struggles with ADD, dyslexia, or other learning disabilities and doesn't fit the typical classroom, or the kid who doesn't see the need for school and doesn't take it seriously. We can take each challenge and pray like crazy about it.

School will offer different challenges to different kids based on their personalities, learning styles, and interests. As parents, we can recognize the specific challenges our children face and pray for them.

## Pray for their Sabbath School

School isn't the only place our children go to learn. Church, Sabbath School, and youth group are also learning places. They create a whole new list of things to pray for. Often for younger children, church is a fun place they love to attend. As they grow older, they often become

bored with church and youth group. In smaller churches, there may not be much offered for youth and young adults. Those who volunteer to teach may not know how to reach the disinterested young people sitting in their classrooms looking bored or giggling and whispering to their friends.

Lift up these teachers and leaders in prayer. Ask God to give them wisdom and ideas, a heart for the kids, and a desire to make the lesson not only real, but fun.

We've often been a part of churches that haven't had many young people. So I've prayed for God to send other youth, for Him to help my sons connect to older people as well, and to send people who will show an interest in them and be a friend no matter what the age. And He's been faithful. We moved to a new church with an active youth group when Josh was a teen. By the time Zach moved into the teen group, most of the young people had moved away. There were a lot of weeks when it was just him or only another kid or two. Yet God connected him to two of his teachers. One of those teachers loved cars even more than Zach did. He took Zach to car shows and races and made a point to talk to him each week. His other teacher was a good friend of mine who would take time to talk to Zach when he'd answer her phone calls to our house.

> What our children experience in church and youth group will influence their attitude toward God and Christians and can influence whether they continue to attend church as young adults.

When my sons showed signs of losing interest in church and not wanting to go, I prayed that God would work in them and help them find a place where they felt they fit, as well as bring them friends to hang out with. I prayed that

He would help them to hear what He desired them to hear, if they weren't really listening, or help them to find a new place to worship.

Recently, I joined a few other moms who were concerned that their young adult children were really not feeling a part of church and were no longer wanting to attend faithfully. We began praying and committed to fasting for one week together as another friend worked on putting together a new church plant that would be designed specifically for that group. When Grace Outlet launched, Zach went with me to check it out. The leader had been the camp pastor during Zach's summer camp experience and was already someone Zach respected. He enjoyed the more relaxed atmosphere and the practical sermons. It became a place he wanted to go to, a place where he slowly began meeting other kids his age and developing friendships.

What our children experience in church and youth group will influence their attitude toward God and Christians and can influence whether they continue to attend church as young adults. It's a very important area of their lives for us as parents to pray like crazy about.

## What if they're homeschooled?

If we are our kids' teachers and their classroom is a room in our house, we still need to pray, especially for ourselves as teachers—that God will guide our planning and curriculum and that He will guide us not only as we teach, but also as we parent, and for that balance of discipline and fun, that we not only see the teachable moments, but also the opportunities to laugh, have fun, play, and just hang out without having to do anything.

We can also pray that God brings the extracurricular activities that our children may want and need—social opportunities, field trips, classes that they're interested in but that we may not want to or be able to teach. We will

know all too well the challenges they face in learning (or the challenges they create) and pray specifically for those challenges and wisdom in how to overcome them for both of us.

We can ask God to help them to find friends with similar values and interests, which may be harder when they're learning at home instead of school, but is an important part of their lives.

Education is a huge part of our children's lives. It's an area to continually pray like crazy for, as God teaches them and guides them into the next step of their lives.

One of the reasons many parents homeschool isn't primarily academic, but spiritual. They want to give their children a solid foundation and to disciple them as they grow. We can make it a primary prayer request that God will help us keep in focus that our goal is not just for them to learn and grow academically. We can ask Him to consistently remind us that we want more than just good test results; we want to teach our children how to include God in every activity, every part of their lives, and choose to live for Him. We can pray that He will help us to live a good example, helping us not to become angry, become frustrated, or be critical or negative. Homeschooled kids are seeing their parents 24/7, at their best and worst. We need God's guidance in every one of those moments, as much as or more than those who teach kids during the day and then send them back to their parents.

## Pray for wisdom as they make decisions for the future

After years and years of school, of getting up on cold winter mornings and making that trip to get them there, and of fighting the homework battle so often that I just wanted to give up, graduation did come, and with it a new chapter in each of our sons' lives. A new area to pray for: their decisions on what to do next. Will they go to college? Which one? What will they major in? If not college, a trade school or technical school? Perhaps not school but instead settle into an apprenticeship? Or take a year off to decide? Several of Josh's and Zach's friends chose to take a year off and serve as student missionaries first. A few chose to get married shortly after graduation.

As parents, we can pray for and with our kids as they make these decisions, asking God to give them wisdom, praying that He will show them His will and purpose clearly, and praying that they will discover their passions and talents and ways for using those in a career that they will enjoy and be able to provide for their future.

Education is a huge part of our children's lives. It's an area to continually pray like crazy for, as God teaches them and guides them into the next step of their lives.

## Pray for:

1. their school to be a safe place for them to learn;
2. the administration to make good decisions;
3. the school board as they hire teachers and set policies;
4. their schoolwork and assignments;
5. challenges they face;
6. their classmates to know and love God;
7. their teachers personally—and that they see the potential in your children;
8. sports/teams to be a good and positive experiences;
9. extracurricular activities that will help enhance their education and show them possibilities for future careers and education;

10. the choices they need to make as they decide on colleges and majors;
11. their Sabbath School class/youth group leaders to be passionate about young people and about God;
12. godly Christian teens for them to hang out with at church;
13. places of worship where they feel accepted and are places they can grow and serve;
14. you as a parent and a teacher of your homeschool;
15. and extracurricular activities and social opportunities through which homeschooled kids can meet other kids with shared values and interests.

## Journal

- How have you seen God lead your children in their education?
- Who are the teachers and administrators of your children's schools for whom you would like to pray? (Many schools have a Web site that lists staff if you'd like to get names that you don't already have.)
- If you are homeschooling your children, what are your specific prayer needs?
- Write a prayer for yourself as their teacher and principal.
- What are the specific challenges that your children face in school that you want to or are making a matter of prayer?
- Write a prayer about these challenges now.
- In what extracurricular activities are your children involved? What are things you are or will be praying about these activities?

## Praying for the Places They Learn

- Write a prayer for them.
- What classes are your children taking? What do they enjoy? What do they dislike? How can you be praying for their classes?
- Write a prayer for their classes and assignments.
- Are your children making decisions for college? How will you be praying for that?
- Who are their Sabbath School teachers? Their pastor? Who and how will you pray for their Christian education experience?
- Write a prayer for these teachers and spiritual leaders.
- Claim a scripture passage, personalize it, and write it as a prayer for your children: Psalm 25:4, 5; Proverbs 22:6; Isaiah 50:4.
- Keep a record of other scripture passages you want to personalize and claim for your children.

# Praying for Purpose

*I know the thoughts that I think toward you, says the Lord, thoughts of peace and not of evil, to give you a future and a hope.—Jeremiah 29:11*

From the time Zach was about four years old, he knew what he wanted to be. We had read the biography of Ben Carson, who quickly became one of his heroes, and the biography of Dave Dravecky, the pitcher who had cancer, which detailed some of the surgeries he received on his shoulder. The stories inspired him to want to become a heart surgeon. He mapped out his career plans at a very young age. Medical school at Loma Linda University in Southern California and interning at John Hopkins University, where Dr. Carson works. Then he would begin his practice in Tennessee, a state he learned had a good educational payback plan for doctors.

Zach talked about it like it was an inevitable reality. He would be a heart surgeon. He'd be rich and, once he had his own practice well established, would be able to limit his time at work so that he could have plenty of time for his family. (Though he often talked about how in the "early years" his wife would have to do a lot of the family stuff alone, including chopping wood for the woodstove, because he'd "be at the hospital.")

It was funny to watch adults ask this little kid what he wanted to be when he grew up, knowing they were expecting him to say, "a fireman" or "a baseball player," only to have him say, "I'm going to be a heart surgeon, and I'm going to get my medical degree from Loma Linda University."

He knew his purpose.

Then came the teen years, and suddenly he wasn't so sure. What did he want to be? What did God want for his life? What did God create him to do?

He's still not totally sure.

Josh was the more typical little boy. He wanted to be a baseball player for a while, then moved on to something else, and then something else. It was always something different, depending on what interested him at that moment of his life. After school, he explored various options—construction jobs, classes in communication, considering a major in environmental science, and art.

I continually pray that God will give each of our sons a sense of the purpose He has for them. That He will show them how to look at their gifts, talents, and interests and how to use them.

Through it all, I've been praying.

I continually pray that God will give each of our sons a sense of the purpose He has for them. That He will show them how to look at their gifts, talents, and interests and how to use them. His Word tells us that He has plans for them, a purpose, and specific thoughts about them. A sense of purpose is what keeps a person going and motivates us to do what needs to be done. It gives our lives meaning. I want those things for my sons. I pray and ask God to help them know these things, to discover their purpose in Him and not in other things, and to find meaning in living for Him.

## Passion

While Zachary no longer wants to be a heart surgeon and may not be sure of his purpose, he does know what his

biggest passion is: cars. He reads magazine after magazine about cars. He is full of all kinds of information about cars, and can tell you the make, model, and year of a car by looking at it. (And has tried to teach his mom to recognize at least make and models, to no avail.) His MySpace page has videos of cars doing burnouts. He already owns two vehicles, a practical one for driving and a Camaro that's currently sitting on blocks as he continues to work on it. One year, he even bought a candle at a car show that smelled like burning rubber when lighted. Cars are his passion.

I long for them to be passionate about God, so I ask God to pour that in them . . . that He will give them each a passion for the things He wants them to be passionate about.

While as a female I don't totally understand, I pray that God will show him how to use that passion for Him. And I also pray that God will give Zach a passion for the other things God desires him to have a passion for. One of my regular prayers is that God will give each of my guys "purpose and passion." I long for them to be passionate about God, so I ask God to pour that in them and that He will give them each a passion for the things He wants them to be passionate about.

## Using it all for Him

I've always wanted my sons to have more than just a job, more than just a place they go to every day to earn money. I long for them to have careers that not only give them a sense of satisfaction and that they can enjoy, but I want them to be where God has created them to be, using their passions, gifts, and talents in a way that brings God glory. So I pray for those things. I ask God to guide them as they choose jobs and that He will direct their paths to where

He wants them to be. I know He has created them unique, with their own blend of personality, talent, and abilities, and will use that combination to do big and little things for Him. I've reminded my sons of it all their lives. "God has a plan for you. He's created you for something special." I've attempted to help them look at what they're passionate about and what they're good at and ways for using those passions and talents in a career—and prayed that God would show them and help them to do what it takes to get there.

## Motivate them, Lord!

All through high school, Josh worked on a horse farm. It was a race horse baby farm, basically. Thoroughbred mares came there to give birth. The babies stayed on the farm until they were yearlings or three years old. They could have up to a hundred horses on the farm at a time. It was a good experience for Josh.

The owners loved him. He was their jack-of-all-trades. He could fix the vacuum cleaner in the house, lead the horses to the fields, drive the water cart around filling water barrels, spread stone in the lunging ring, repair the golf carts they drove everywhere, and do just about anything else they needed him to do.

Over the years, they genuinely came to care about him and what was best for him. So when he had been out of school for a while with no clear plan on what to do next, they decided to "help" motivate him to take the next step. They knew how much he hated painting, so they began giving him nothing but painting jobs, one right after the other. It was the summer when all the barns "needed" a fresh coat of paint. (His boss told me this story herself.)

It worked. He got frustrated enough that he found a new job and a direction that would lead him to a stronger future in the job market.

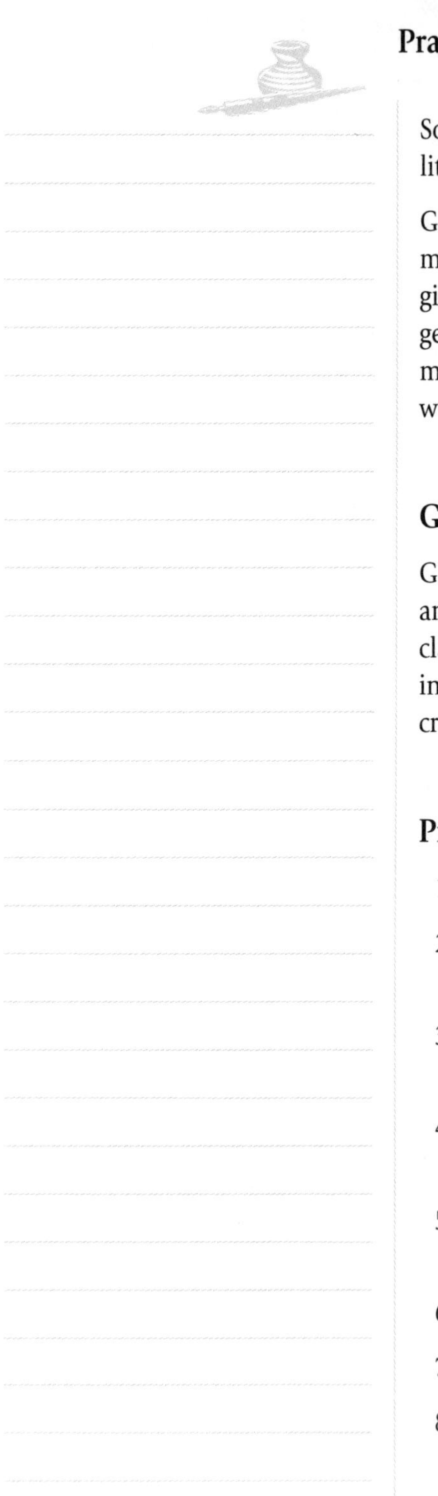

Sometimes our kids need a little motivation. They need a little push to take the next step, the nudge to get moving.

God can nudge them better than I can. So I ask Him to motivate them, to show them what the next step is and give them the desire to do it, to give them what it takes to get where they need to be, and when necessary, He will make them unhappy enough with where they are that it will push them to take the next step.

## God's future for them

God promises that He has a plan that includes a future and a hope. Good things, not evil. As parents, we can claim those promises and pray them back to God, expecting that He will guide our kids into being and doing all He created them for.

## Pray for:

1. them to discover God's purpose for their lives;
2. them to discover ways to use their talents and gifts for God through their jobs;
3. them to know the jobs and careers that God has created them for;
4. clarity as they discover God's will and desires for their lives;
5. motivation to do what it takes to pursue their purpose and passion;
6. vision;
7. God to give them a passion for Him;
8. and God to give them a passion for the things He wants them to do.

## Journal

- How have you seen God lead your children to use their gifts and talents for His purpose?
- How are you praying, or will you pray, for your children to know God's purpose?
- Write out a prayer for your children to discover God's purpose for their lives.
- What are the special gifts and talents you see in your children?
- Write a prayer thanking God for those gifts and talents and asking Him to show them how to use their talents for Him.
- What things are your children passionate about?
- Pray and commit those passions to God, asking Him to use them, and asking Him to create a deeper passion for Him in their lives.
- What impressed you about this chapter? What would you like to begin praying for your children, as a result?
- Personalize and claim a scripture passage for your children: Deuteronomy 10:12; Jeremiah 29:11; Romans 12:1, 2.
- What other scriptures would you like to claim and personalize for your children?

# Praying for Love

As seniors, both Josh and Zach had to take "family and individual studies" at their high school. It was a class that taught responsibilities, had them carry around babies for a week, and assigned a number of papers that required them to talk to other family members before they could be written.

One of those assignments required the student to talk to a parent about love and marriage. They had to ask, "What do you want to see in a spouse for me? What age do you think a person needs to be before he or she should get married?" and other questions designed to get parents and kids talking about love and the commitment of marriage.

I was the parent they both chose to interview.

I don't remember Josh's paper, but I remember finding Zach's completed project on the kitchen table and enjoyed reading it. When he got to the section asking what the parent was wanting for them to find in a spouse, he had written, "I already knew what my mom was going to say before I asked her, and I was right. . . ."

I had to laugh.

It was true. They both knew that I wanted them to marry godly Christian women who would be their best friends, who would encourage them and dream dreams for them, and help them to be all God had created them to be. I had told them so often that they probably could almost have written my words verbatim. But I had told God even more often.

## More than just marriage

I began praying for their future spouses from the moment

they were born. I prayed throughout their lives that God would even then be with these young women and be growing them into His daughters and the plans He had for them, that He would be preparing them to meet my sons and to be their best friends. I prayed for their protection and that God would bless them richly, that He would make them beautiful from the inside out—women who knew how to have fun, laugh, encourage, and dream.

Neither of my sons are married yet. In those moments when they're not seriously dating but would like to be and don't understand why they're not, I've jokingly told them that it's my fault. I've set the bar too high and made it hard for God. I've asked for a lot. They just laugh and know that I want so very much for them.

I began praying for their future spouses from the moment they were born . . . that God would . . . be with these young women . . . growing them into His daughters.

I pray for more than just their future spouses, but also for every woman they will date, that God will use each relationship and experience to teach them and help them grow as men, that He will help them to know how to treat a woman, to remain pure, to respect her and value her, and that each relationship will be a part of learning how to have a friendship with a woman. Men and women are different. How we relate as friends is different. I've always encouraged my sons to be just friends with girls, assuring them that those relationships would help them when they did date and eventually marry.

When they are in a dating relationship, I pray specifically for the person that they're dating. As they tell me things about them, about what's happening in their lives, the decisions they need to make, and anything else, I pray specifically for those things. And if appropriate, I've told

the girls that I'm praying for them. I've grown a friendship with one young woman Zach has been seriously dating. We sometimes e-mail each other or talk in person, and she has shared specific things she'd like me to pray about and has followed up to tell me how things turned out. I've invited her out to lunch and have developed a friendship with her. This is a little tricky because I now have a relationship with someone I care about and am praying for. If she and my son break up or have a problem, it will impact my relationship with her. But I can continue to pray for her regardless.

## Broken hearts happen

As all young people, my sons have had their share of broken hearts, betrayals, and breakups. It is so hard parenting this age sometimes! I just hate to see my child's heart get broken. I want to prevent it, or fix it.

While there's little you can do to prevent or fix broken hearts, you can pray. Ask God to bring healing for both your children and the ones they broke up with and that God will guide and give them wisdom in waiting to date again and in how to handle being around or seeing the previous girlfriends or boyfriends.

While there's little you can do to prevent or fix broken hearts, you can pray. Ask God to bring healing for both your children and the ones they broke up with.

This can be even more difficult if your child is an adult and going through a divorce. It's even more painful if grandchildren are involved. Yet we can trust our children, no matter what their ages or circumstance, to God. Pray for them. Pray for their previous spouse. Pray for the grandchildren. Pray for the relationship between your child and the parent of his or her children, that they

can work together to raise their children the best they can separately.

Sometimes we may want to do more, but offering a listening ear, a hug, and our prayers—both for them and, when possible, with them—are big things to do and will help more than we can know.

## And not just for the other person

While I have always prayed for the women they will marry and each of those they will date or are dating, I have also prayed for my sons, that God will help them to be godly Christian men who will treat women with respect, wait for sex until marriage, learn how to be a friend, and to support and encourage and dream dreams for the one God chooses for them and all those they date along the way. I pray they will be husbands who will help their wives be all God created them to be, who will support their dreams and efforts, and who will truly listen and attempt to understand.

## And once they're married . . .

Our family is preparing for a wedding. No, not one of my sons. My niece and her fiancé are getting married in July. Her mom is making the dress. Both parents have been experimenting with fondant for the cake. The wedding is scheduled to happen in a park on a summer day in July.

I know my brother and his wife are praying like crazy.

Marriage is a big step. Marriage is hard.

There are days when you're madly in love and days when you wonder if you were ever in love. Days when life is good and days when you wonder if you made a mistake.

As our children grow and marry, their marriages and spouses are another addition to our prayer lists. They may

move out of our houses and set up homes for themselves, but they still need our support, especially our prayer support.

While we're not there yet, I know that once my sons are married, I will consistently be praying for their marriages, for their spouses, and for them as husbands.

## Not everyone will marry

But not all our children will marry, and many who do may wait until later in life. As parents, we can pray that God will guide them in their singleness and to keep them pure and content. Some choose singleness as a way of life because it is what they want. Others don't choose to be single, don't even want to be single, but haven't found the right guy or gal yet. While we will continue to pray that if it's God's will, He will guide them to that right person, we can in the meantime pray that God will use this time in their lives for good, that He will teach them and develop who they are, growing them into responsible and independent young adults, or older adults, who find their completion in Him alone.

> As our children grow and marry, their marriages and spouses are another addition to our prayer lists. They may move out of our houses and set up homes for themselves, but they still need our . . . prayer support.

## Love is hard

As I watch my sons date and watch their friends date and marry, I am thankful that I am not young and single! I would not want to be dating and looking for a mate in today's world. It looks just too hard and often too painful. I am constantly

reminded that this is an area I need to be praying about daily for my sons, that God will guide them, protect them, and help them to make wise choices. Choosing a spouse will be a life-altering decision. Even if the marriage ends in divorce, that relationship will be a permanent part of their lives. Even if their marriage doesn't end in divorce, marriage is hard. They need God to be a part of every relationship and especially a part of their marriage.

## Pray for:

1. God to bring them a godly Christian spouse;
2. God to work in the life of their future spouse right now, preparing them, guiding them, and growing them into the person He desires them to be;
3. God to guide in the lives and choices of all the people they'll date and/or are the person they're currently dating to know God and to know His purpose;
4. God to guide them in their relationships and to keep them sexually pure;
5. their marriage—that God will be the center of it and guide them, bringing them closer to each other and to Him;
6. our single children to be content and to have peace as a single person;
7. healing when relationships end;
8. and couples who divorce to be able to work through their relationships, especially if they have children together so that they can raise those children together to the best of their ability.

## Journal

- Have you seen God lead in your children's dating and marriage? If so, how?
- How did God lead in your own life during dating and marriage?
- How you pray for your children in this topic depends on their stage of life. When they're young is a good time to begin praying for their dating relationships and their future spouses. When they're dating, it's important to pray specifically for their relationships and the decisions they are making together—for the influence that the relationship has on their futures. If your children are already married, praying for their spouses and children, if there any, can help add support and strength. If they've been through a divorce, you can pray for healing and future relationships. Depending on which stage your children are in, how will you, or are you, praying for them and their love relationships?
- Based on how this chapter has impressed you or on what you've taken away from it, write out a prayer for your children.
- Claim and personalize a scripture passage for your children: 1 Corinthians 13:4–7; Ephesians 5:21–33. Write it out as a prayer for them.
- What other scripture passages do you want to personalize and claim?

# Praying for Who They Are

My mom had five kids. I'm the oldest and the only girl. The youngest of the four boys was born when I was only four and a half. Needless to say, we were pretty close in age. Yet we were totally different from each other.

I was the girly-girl. I loved to play with dolls and play house and dress up. I loved to read and enjoyed school. (I think I was the only one who enjoyed school.) I was involved in everything: at school I was in the band, chorus, and student council; I wrote for the school paper; and I joined over half a dozen committees and clubs—as well as running track one year and always trying out but never making cheerleading. At church I was one of the peer leaders of our youth group.

Nile was born when I was ten months old. He has always been the strong, silent type. He's a hard worker who has often worked several jobs at a time all his life. My parents often commented that he never played as a kid. He just worked. Today he's the parent of two young-adult daughters who are definitely girly-girls. His house is full of giggling and noise, and he has learned to play and joke around. Mom now says that it took him until he was an adult to learn how to be a kid. (God sure has a sense of humor, giving Nile girls and me boys!)

Darren is the middle kid. He's the charmer who could talk his way into and out of anything. Teachers loved him even if he wasn't the most committed student. He had the ability to be talking as if he wasn't paying attention, yet be completely aware of everything that was going on. One time Dad was showing Nile how to tear apart an engine and put it back together again. Darren was right there,

talking nonstop as they worked. He didn't seem to be paying any attention to what they were doing. But as they began putting the engine back together again, Darren amazed Dad by knowing what part went where.

Kent was the quiet type, though you might not believe that now. Today he can keep up with Darren when it comes to talking and telling stories. When he was little, he loved to read, one time reading the most books in the library's summer reading program. He also loved animals. We lived on a small farm, and Kent seemed to collect the pets that were the most unusual, such as Hermit crabs and turtles. While Nile and Darren were riding the horses and feeding calves, Kent was enjoying filling aquariums with gerbils and fish. He's one of those guys who would give you the shirt off his back, even if you were a complete stranger.

Byron was the baby of the family and the most quiet. He didn't talk a lot. He loved cars and drawing. He collected Matchbox cars and spent hours putting models together, but not the way the instructions on the box suggested. He'd take parts from this model and from that one and another one and build something unique. His architecture teacher in high school said he was one of the most gifted students he had ever taught. I sometimes wonder what he would've gone on to achieve if his life hadn't been cut short when he was still a high-school senior.

Five kids. Same parents. Totally different people. Even as grown-ups today, our differences outnumber our similarities. We are all deeply committed to our families. Three of us are actively involved in our church communities. We are all hard working and dependable people, respected in the places we work. And these days, all four of us are talkers. But we are still very different from each other. Nile's family spends their vacations camping in campgrounds and enjoying the activities there. He loves hunting and riding his motorcycle with his wife. They're learning the fun of an empty nest together. Darren still has four kids at home. They enjoy weekends in their cabin at the lake. His home

is always full of other kids. He's been a Boy Scout leader, a "stable dad" when his oldest daughter was taking riding lessons, and serves on the school board of his kids' Christian school. Kent and his wife enjoy spending their weekends babysitting their granddaughter. (They're the only grandparents in the bunch.) They head to the beach for rare vacations, and both work six or seven days a week much too often. None of my brothers understand my love for writing or speaking, though they're proud of their big sister, and they can't understand the pleasure Tim and I get from hiking to the tops of mountains.

No matter how many kids you have, they're all different, each one with his or her own personality and characteristics.

It's the same story with any family. No matter how many kids you have, they're all different, each one with his or her own personality and characteristics, even for twins.

## Different kids, different prayers

Josh and Zach are totally different kids. Their differences have actually increased as they've grown older. As I pray for their unique personalities and characteristics, for their habits, my prayers are different for each one.

Josh is social. Zach is more independent. That has influenced how I've prayed for them. Sometimes Josh has copied friends too much. At times Zach hasn't spent enough time developing friends. I've prayed specifically for each one based on who they are.

Zachary sees the world as black and white. That's a good strength, but sometimes I've needed to pray for his attitude toward people and situations because he saw it too black and white and didn't empathize enough. Josh is the opposite. He sees almost everything in grays and has incredible

empathy for people. A caring heart, but sometimes I've needed to pray that he would be firm in what he believes.

Study your kids. Look at their strengths and their weaknesses. Often, their strengths may also be their weaknesses. Pray for them, for God to shape them well. Know their personalities. Are they outgoing or shy? Confident or insecure? Know who they are and pray for the areas they need to grow in. Thank God for their strengths. Ask Him to convict them on the things that need changing and then to give them strength, courage, and motivation to change. Pray that He will bring the people and situations into their lives that will help shape who they are the way God desires.

Study your kids. Look at their strengths and their weaknesses. Often, their strengths may also be their weaknesses. Pray for them, for God to shape them well.

## A wise man's request

God went to Solomon and offered him whatever he'd like. God was going to grant his request. Solomon didn't ask for riches or fame. Instead, he asked for wisdom, understanding, and largeness of heart (1 Kings 3:9; 2 Chronicles 1:10). God granted his request and gave him riches and honor as well. Solomon was known for his wisdom.

These sounded like good requests for me to pray for as well. So I added them to the list of the things I've often prayed for in regard to my sons, that God would give them wisdom, understanding, and largeness of heart. (The original language is more accurately translated a "hearing" heart.) James 1:5 also promises that if anyone lacks wisdom, just ask and God will give wisdom liberally and without reproach. I have asked that God give my sons wisdom, understanding, and largeness of heart toward God, that they would know and understand Him.

## Other good characteristics

As you read the Bible, you may discover many things that are good to ask God to give your children as you pray for the people that they are and the people they are growing to be. I have often used Bible passages as the basis for prayer requests for my sons. And I have looked for the qualities the Bible talks about a person needing and have prayed for those very qualities in my children.

God repeatedly told Joshua to be strong and courageous, so I pray for my own Joshua and for Zachary, that God will help them to be strong and courageous.

Paul wrote that he had learned to be content no matter what. I've asked God to teach my children to be content in all situations and with who they are—their gifts and talents and abilities.

Jesus promises peace that passes understanding, an abundant life, and joy that is full. Each of these promises is a prompt to me to prayerfully claim these characteristics for my children, that God will fill them with peace, that He will give them an abundant life and not just a let's-get-through-the-day life, and that He will fill their hearts with joy.

Thank God for their strengths. Ask Him to convict them on the things that need changing and then to give them strength, courage, and motivation to change.

The Bible encourages us to come before God's throne with boldness, so I ask God to give my sons boldness and the belief that they can come to Him with anything, knowing that He hears and cares. I pray that Zack and Josh will have the boldness to be who they are and know that is exactly who they are to be. I've asked Him to fill them with confidence, that in this world where we question ourselves,

put ourselves down, compare ourselves to others, and come up short, they will learn to not only appreciate but like and value the person God has created them to be.

## Pray for:

1. God to mold their characters and personality;
2. Him to convict them of bad habits and help them to change;
3. God to give them wisdom;
4. God to give them understanding;
5. God to give them largeness of heart that Solomon requested;
6. Him to bless them with contentedness;
7. Him to give them confidence and boldness;
8. God to protect who He's created them to be;
9. and them to like and value the person He's created them to be.

## Journal

- Journal a bit about each of your children—who they are, what they're like, their unique characteristics.
- What are their strengths?
- Write a prayer of thanks for those strengths.
- What are their weaknesses?
- Write a prayer about those weaknesses.
- What characteristics would you like to pray for them to acquire?
- Write out a prayer for these.

## Praying for Who They Are

- What impressed you in this chapter? What will you take away and include in your prayer time for your children?
- Claim and personalize a scripture passage for your children: Joshua 1:7; Philippians 4:11; Galatians 5:22, 23; James 1:5. Write it out as a prayer.
- What other scripture passages would you like to claim?

# Praying About Sin

My kids aren't perfect.

They make mistakes. They have bad habits. I don't know about Josh's home now that he lives on his own, but Zach's room is still a mess. They've been known to drive too fast. And that's just scratching the surface.

My kids are sinners. The Bible says that all have sinned and fallen short of the glory of God (Romans 3:23). This description includes my sons.

I don't expect perfection from them. I know they're going to sin, make bad choices and mistakes, and do things that I've taught them are wrong.

As a parent, I've attempted to teach my children right from wrong. But I also rely on the Holy Spirit to convict them of right and wrong, as well. It is part of the work He does in each of our hearts.

## Right and wrong

As a parent, I've attempted to teach my children right from wrong. But I also rely on the Holy Spirit to convict them of right and wrong, as well. It is part of the work He does in each of our hearts, helping us to know what to do and what not to do. We can pray and give Him permission to convict our children of right and wrong, asking Him to give the desire to do right and cause sin to look distasteful.

When I know specific sins of my children, I pray specifically that God will convict them of the sin and make it distasteful and that God will give them the desire to not do it anymore.

## A Bible father's example

The Bible tells us that Job was a godly man, "blameless and upright, and one who feared God and shunned evil" (Job 1:1). He was also a father. He had seven sons and three daughters.

He was a dad who knew his kids were sinners. And he prayed for them. He didn't know for sure what they were doing, but he knew that they might sin, and so he offered sacrifices for them, "Thus Job did regularly" (verse 5). He regularly offered sacrifices for his children in case they sinned.

He provides an example for us as parents. We can pray for our children, asking God to forgive them of their sins.

## Jesus' example

When the disciples asked Jesus to teach them how to pray, He taught them to pray about sin. " 'Forgive us our debts, / As we forgive our debtors. / And do not lead us into temptation / But deliver us from the evil one' " (Matthew 6:12, 13).

We can pray for our children, that not only will God forgive their sins, but that He will give them strength to avoid temptation—strength to walk away when temptation comes.

While Jesus' prayer teaches us to pray for the forgiveness of sin, it also gives us the example to pray that God will help us to avoid temptation and deliver us from the evil one. These, too, are examples of things we can pray for our children, that not only will God forgive their sins, but that He will give them strength to avoid temptation—strength to walk away when temptation comes.

The evil one, the devil, is out to destroy our children. No

matter how young or old they are, he wants to lead them away from God and into sin. There truly is a battle going on for our children. "Deliver us from the evil one" prompts me to pray that God will keep the devil from my sons, that He will bind him away from them, and that my sons will choose God's will in this battle.

## Accepting God's forgiveness

The devil is relentless. If he loses one battle, he'll just start another. When our children (or we) are convicted of sin, confess it, and walk away, the devil will tempt us to do it again. If he can't win that battle, he'll try to discourage us by reminding us of our unworthiness because of our sin. He'll beat us up through his lies, wanting us to believe that we're hopeless, that God can't possibly forgive us again if we fall into sin again, that God can't use us because of our past sin, or whatever lies he can get us to hear and believe that will defeat us.

His strategy works on us, and it works on our children.

It's another part of the battle we fight on our knees for our kids, praying that they will not only be convicted and confess, but that they will accept the forgiveness that God offers and live it, and forgive themselves. I met a young man once who knew God had forgiven him of his sin, but he couldn't forgive himself. His past sin continued to eat at him and cause him to beat himself up relentlessly. That is not what God wants for us or our children. That's not where I want my sons to live. So I pray that God will help them to let go of their past sins and mistakes and to live in His forgiveness, that they will ignore the lies of the devil and know that there is hope, know that they have value, and know that God will use them regardless.

## Battling for our children

The battle for our children is very real. The devil will do

everything in his power to defeat them and take them away from God. He hates our kids.

> God . . . loves our children and will do everything in His power to draw them to Him and help them to live as He planned.

God, on the other hand, loves our children and will do everything in His power to draw them to Him and help them to live as He planned.

We're a part of that battle as we pray like crazy that God will convict our children of their sins, forgive them, and give them the strength to change and the courage to believe that they are forgiven.

## Pray for:

1. strength against temptation;
2. forgiveness of sins;
3. God to convict them of right and wrong;
4. God to give them the desire to do right;
5. God to convict them of sins and give them the desire to change;
6. and for them to accept God's forgiveness and not beat themselves up over their sin.

## Journal

- How has God helped you overcome sin and/or temptation? Write about an experience, thanking God for how He has taught you and led you.
- Are there areas in which your children struggle that you

want to commit to or have committed to prayer?

- Write out a prayer about this struggle.
- What impressed you in this chapter? What would you like to take away and incorporate in your prayer life for your children?
- Personalize and claim a scripture promise for your children: Matthew 6:12, 13; 1 Corinthians 10:13; James 1:12; 1 John 1:9.
- What other scripture passages would you like to claim for your children?

# Praying for Parenting

I've been a parent for over twenty-three years. It's been an adventure that has taught me much about myself, about God's love, and about prayer. Probably nothing else in my life has caused me to pray more fervently or get on my knees more often than praying like crazy for my kids. Not a day goes by that I'm not taking them to God for one reason or another, even if it's just to thank Him for them and to again beg Him to be real to them and to give them a hunger for Him.

Probably nothing else in my life has caused me to pray more fervently or get on my knees more often than praying like crazy for my kids.

While it's true that I have prayed like crazy for them, I have also prayed like crazy for myself as their parent. As I shared in the first chapter, the thought of being responsible for a baby struck fear in my heart. I knew I had no idea what I was doing and that the only way I could be a good parent was with God's help every step of the way.

### The kind of parent you want to be

Before Josh was born, I talked to God about the kind of parent I wanted to be. I made a list in my mind, defining what parenting would look like for me. I realize now that I was simply creating a vision of what my parenting would look like. I told God that I wanted to be the kind of parent who said "I love you" every day. I wanted to hug and snuggle and make sure my kids knew they were loved unconditionally. I also wanted to play with them, read to them, and spend time with them. I chose to be a stay-at-home mom

and asked God to remind me constantly that I didn't stay home so I could clean the house or volunteer in the community, but so that I could raise my kids, teach them, play with them, and nurture them. I asked God to make me the kind of parent who listened—that my children would always know that I cared about whatever was on their hearts. I prayed that He would give me wisdom and patience, two things I've had to ask Him for over and over again.

God has honored those requests.

I am not the perfect parent, but my sons know without a doubt that I love them. We have close relationships. I know they don't tell me everything, but am glad to see that they feel they can talk to me about anything. (Zach even recently prefaced something he told me by saying, "Probably as my mom you don't want to know this, but . . .") It doesn't mean that when they've told me something they haven't sometimes received some motherly advice.

God has continued to expand my vision for the kind of parent I want Him to enable me to be.

We have played together, built forts together, gone Rollerblading together, played baseball together, have created things with Legos together, played Scrabble and Monopoly and other games together, and we've read hundreds of books together—during one week of winter blizzards, we read the entire Little House on the Prairie series in a matter of days.

We have laughed, and cried, and even battled a bit.

And God has continued to expand my vision for the kind of parent I want Him to enable me to be.

## God knows and loves them more

I love my sons fiercely. Just the thought of them right now

brings a smile to my face. Josh's dark eyes with that twinkle and the smile that just melts my heart. Zach's stories and sense of humor. Such handsome men!

It's hard for me to really comprehend that God knows and loves them even more than I do. Yet I know He does.

So I pray and ask Him to give me understanding of who my sons are and what they're about and what's going on in their lives and hearts. I pray that He will help me see them the way He does, through His eyes. I ask Him to give me wisdom in nurturing their unique personalities and to help me parent each one of them in the way he needs to be trained. I've never been a parent who has to do for one what I did for the other to keep things even and fair. (Kids will probably always find reasons to say a parent isn't fair!) Instead, I've asked for the ability to parent each child individually and uniquely in ways that will help nurture, equip, and challenge him to be who God created him to be.

### Make it fun, God!

Parenting is hard work. There are a lot of frustrating times, difficult tasks, and times when your children are angry with you and may even tell you that they don't like you, even tell you that they hate you. Parenting can be a very unpopular job.

We can pray for strength and courage to do the right thing, even if our kids don't understand or become angry.

In those moments, we can pray for strength and courage to do the right thing, even if our kids don't understand or become angry. Admittedly, I want my sons to like me. Yet at the same time, it's more important for me to do what's best for them, discipline when it's needed, assign chores and responsibilities, even though they get mad, and set rules

and guidelines such as curfews and no television until homework is done.

Yet I also pray and ask God to help me to laugh and be fun and enjoy my children and to help me see it as more than just a job and a responsibility but a pleasure—fun. I want my sons to know that I enjoy them, and I want them to grow up with memories of our having fun together and laughing often.

## Someday they'll be parents

Both my sons have always talked about wanting to be parents someday. They both want sons. (They think girls are a bit too dramatic.) Zach looks forward to talking to his son about cars and taking him fishing. Josh will probably teach his children to love the outdoors the way he does. I'm sure his family will spend a bit of time hiking and camping.

When they become parents, we can support them in prayer. Praying for them as parents the way we've prayed for ourselves as parents. Or if we didn't pray for ourselves, pray for them the way we wish someone had been praying for us. Asking God to give them wisdom, laughter, patience, and fun, praying that God will teach them much about His love and His character through their experience as parents. (There are some things you just don't understand until you've parented.)

We can also support them in prayer as parents by praying for their children, our grandchildren, praying for them in the same way we've prayed for our children (or wish we had prayed for our children) throughout their lives.

## It's a never-ending job

Parenting is a job that never ends. From the moment of conception, our hearts are captured and our responsibility grows. Even after our children have grown up and moved out on their own, we continue to be parents. I heard someone say recently that when your own parents die, you become an orphan. When your marriage ends, you become single again. But there is no end to parenting. No matter how old your children become, they are still your children. Prayer is one way we continue to carry that responsibility. And when they become parents, the responsibility grows to include new children. It is a responsibility and a privilege to be a part of what God is doing in someone's life by praying for them.

It is a responsibility and a privilege to be a part of what God is doing in someone's life by praying for them.

## Pray for:

1. God to give you wisdom as a parent;
2. patience as a parent;
3. Him to help you see your child as He does;
4. understanding of your child's heart and character;
5. the ability to laugh and have fun and enjoy your child;
6. and all of these for your child as he or she parents.

## Journal

- Remember a particular time that God specifically led you as a parent. Write about it, thanking God for His guidance and for giving you what you needed as a parent.

## Praying Like Crazy for Your Kids

- In what areas do you feel you need God's help as a parent? Write out a prayer for those needs.
- What kind of parent do you want to be? Write a description, but make it present tense. Begin, "I am a parent who . . ." Then write out what you want to be like, how you want to handle things, etc.
- Ask God what He wants you to add to your description. Write down His response.
- Write a prayer asking God to help you be that kind of parent.
- God knows and loves your children even more than you do. Write out a prayer thanking Him for loving them more and doing what's best for them. Ask Him to show you your children the way He sees them.
- What do you enjoy about your children?
- How do you have fun together?
- Thank God for the ability to enjoy your children and ask Him to help you create fun memories together.
- Write out a prayer for your children as parents. If they're not parents yet, for the parents they will be. If they are parents already, pray specifically for needs you know or see, and that God will guide them.
- What has impressed you in this chapter? For what will you begin praying about, or continue praying, for your children?
- Personalize and claim a scripture passages for yourself as a parent: Proverbs 22:6; Ephesians 6:4; Colossians 3:21. Write it out as a prayer.
- What other scripture passages do you want to remember to claim for yourself or for your children?

# Praying Scripture

I love God's Word. I find it powerful and alive. I have several favorite Bibles: my wide-margin New King James Version that I bought with a gift card a church I worked for gave me when I left for a new job. *The Message* Bible that Zachary bought me one Christmas. I already had several different *Message* Bibles—each one containing different parts of the Bible. Zach bought a leather-bound one that not only contained all the books but had chapter and verse markings. He knew how much I enjoyed reading *The Message.* Another smaller New King James Bible sits in the stack by my bed. I've had it since early in our marriage. Its pages are almost a spiritual journal of my walk with God; they're filled with prayers, notes, and promises.

As I read God's Word, I often come across verses that capture just what I'd like to say to God on behalf of my children. So I claim the promises and pray them back to God.

In each of my Bibles, you'll find prayers for my sons written in the margins, sometimes dated, sometimes not. As I read God's Word, I often come across verses that capture just what I'd like to say to God on behalf of my children. So I claim the promises, praying them back to God for the boys. I know that all of God's promises are not only for me and for other adults, but are for our children as well, no matter how young or old and that there is power in praying God's Word back to Him.

Simple promises, such as "I can do all things through Christ who strengthens me," and "My God shall supply all your need according to His riches in glory by Christ Jesus."

## Praying Like Crazy for Your Kids

I pray, "God, enable Josh to do all things through You who strengthens him," or "God, supply all Zach's needs according to Your riches in glory by Christ Jesus."

Many of the prayers in the Bible also capture what I'd love to pray for them, sometimes praying things I wouldn't think of.

Philippians 1:9–11: "And this I pray, that your love may abound still more and more in knowledge and all discernment, that you may approve the things that are excellent, that you may be sincere and without offense till the day of Christ, being filled with the fruits of righteousness which are by Jesus Christ, to the glory and praise of God."

Or the prayer in Colossians 1:9, 10: "For this reason we also, since the day we heard it, do not cease to pray for you, and to ask that you may be filled with the knowledge of His will in all wisdom and spiritual understanding; that you may walk worthy of the Lord, fully pleasing Him, being fruitful in every good work and increasing in the knowledge of God."

I pray the same prayers, inserting my sons' names and personalizing the prayers for them.

Sometimes I pray aloud. Often I just write the date and a note that I'm claiming it for one or both of my sons. Other times I write the prayer in the margin of my Bible. It was one reason I wanted to purchase a wide-margin Bible.

### Sharing it with them

Every year we celebrate the day that each of the boys committed his life to Jesus through baptism. We call it his spiritual birthday. We don't make a cake or have a party, but we do recognize the day, talk about his commitment, and give him a gift that will enhance his walk with God.

This past year, I chose to give both of them the gift of my scripture prayers.

I bought each of them new Bibles. I chose a New Living Translation with a soft, flexible leather cover.

Then I spent several months reading and praying my way through their Bibles. As I prayed, I wrote those prayers in the margins. I highlighted promises I was claiming and wrote prayers claiming those promises for them.

On their spiritual birthdays, I gave them those very marked-up Bibles for their birthdays.

Zach wasn't impressed. He put the Bible on a shelf, and there it sat. I figured that might be his response. I also figured that someday when they were older or after I died, they'd get curious about what I had prayed and would pick the Bibles up and read them. The day came sooner than I thought for Zach. He took the Bible to church with him one week. He and his girlfriend were bored during the service and ended up attempting to read as many of my notes and prayers as they could. Not quite how I expected, but I prayed God would influence both of them through those prayers.

> I believe that the prayers written in those pages are heard not only by God and are being answered daily, but that they will be an example to my sons of how they can pray for others, especially for their own children some day.

Josh's spiritual birthday is on Christmas Day. He was eight years old when he was baptized. He said that his life was the most important gift he could give to Jesus for His birthday. We agreed.

When Josh came home the year I had the Bible wrapped for his spiritual birthday, he told me that he needed me to remind him to take his old Bible back home with him. He wanted it so that he could do some studying. He was at a

place in his life where he was seeking out a few things about God and creation and truth. I was thrilled. I had wondered what he'd think of the new Bible, and now I knew that he *wanted* a Bible. He seemed genuinely pleased. I have no clue if he has read it or not.

Regardless of how they receive it now, I know one day it will be a treasure. And I believe that the prayers written in those pages are heard not only by God and are being answered daily, but that they will be an example to my sons of how they can pray for others, especially for their own children some day.

## Praying Scripture

1. Write the prayers in the margins of your Bible and date them.
2. Write the scripture as a prayer in your own words in a journal.
3. Give them a Bible filled with your prayers and highlighted promises.

## Journal

- What scripture verses has God used to speak to you specifically? How has Scripture blessed you? Journal your thoughts. Add a prayer of thanks to God for His Word and what it means to you.
- What version(s) of the Bible speaks most to you or do you understand best? Have you tried different versions? If not, set a date to go to the bookstore and read your favorite passage through in several versions and purchase the one that resonates the most with your heart. If you don't have dry highlighters (that don't bleed through thin paper) and fine-tip pens (makes writing smaller

easier), purchase several in your favorite colors.

- What are several of your favorite scripture passages?
- Personalize and write them out for both yourself and your children.
- What impressed you the most in this chapter? What one idea or thought will you take away and implement in your life?

# Fasting

*"This kind does not go out except by prayer and fasting." —Matthew 17:21*

He was a father in anguish. His heart was breaking for his son who suffered seizures, and often during an attack, he fell into the fire and was burned or into water, risking drowning. He brought his son to Jesus' disciples and asked them for healing. But they couldn't.

Later the man came to Jesus with his son and again asked for healing. Jesus rebuked the demon, and the child was "cured from that very hour."

The disciples asked Jesus, "Why couldn't we heal him?"

Jesus talked about their unbelief—they doubted that the child truly could be healed—and He concluded by saying, "This kind does not go out except by prayer and fasting" (see Matthew 17:14–21).

There are times when prayer alone is not enough. When praying like crazy means praying and fasting.

## The commitment of fasting

*To fast* is translated from the Hebrew word *tsom* and the Greek word *nesteia* and means "self-denial." Many scholars believe that the practice of fasting began with the loss of appetite during times of great stress or sorrow. We find Hannah weeping and not eating because she was in such distress over being barren (1 Samuel 1:7). She cries out to God during this time, and He answers her prayers with baby Samuel. Scholars believe that fasting became a custom to show deep grief or sorrow, eventually becoming a discipline that demonstrated a deep commitment.

Fasting is a dedication to praying for something you are deeply committed about. It's not your everyday praying. This is the heavy-duty stuff, when there is something you feel so strongly about that it needs more than just prayer.

It may be that your child is involved in something harmful—drinking, drugs, smoking, sex, rebellion, crime, or any other dangerous behavior.

There are times when prayer alone is not enough. When praying like crazy means praying and fasting.

It may be a decision that needs to be made—choosing a college, a major, a job, what to do about a troubled marriage, or any important decision for which you want God's guidance.

You might choose to fast about a habit or character trait you long to see God change, or fast about relationships your child is in—friendships, dating, living together with someone, an abusive person, etc. It may be your child's spiritual walk—especially if he or she is choosing to walk away from God. Whatever causes you incredible stress or when something is heavy on your heart, you can choose to take it to God through prayer and fasting.

## The focus is prayer

There have been moments when I have fasted and prayed specifically for issues in my sons' lives. I have to admit, when I first started fasting, I really didn't understand how to fast. I thought it meant just giving up food. So I'd spend a day not eating. By the end of the day, I'd be pleased with making it through an entire day, but was eagerly waiting the next day when I could eat again; my focus was on the food, eating and not eating. For a long time, I fasted once a week for an entire day. But I didn't truly understand fasting.

## Praying Like Crazy for Your Kids

To fast and pray doesn't mean just giving up food. It means replacing what you're fasting from with prayer. Instead of just skipping meals, take that time when you would normally be eating to pray. It means choosing one thing and replacing it with prayer so that prayer becomes the focus.

### Different types of fast

As I've grown older, I've found that my body responds differently when I try to fast for a whole day. I get a little grouchy. My head hurts. I don't feel well. So I've learned that there are many different ways to fast.

You may completely fast from food for a day or eat one meal—typically either breakfast or dinner—and fast the rest of the day.

These days I typically fast from specific foods, such as chocolate, refined sugars, or iced tea—things I really enjoy and find myself desiring. And when I find myself craving these things, I pray for whatever I'm fasting for instead.

To fast and pray doesn't mean just giving up food. It means replacing what you're fasting from with prayer.

There was a habit of Josh's that I chose to pray and fast about, choosing to give up chocolate. Every time I found myself wanting chocolate, I'd pray for Josh. It was a growing experience for me. I remember being somewhere and getting that craving for chocolate and thinking, *No one will ever know if I indulge this one time; no one is around.* Instantly, the prayer came, "Lord, sometimes Josh is going to be tempted to indulge in this habit because he thinks no one will know. Lord, convict him to be strong, take away the desire, and give him the strength to stand up to temptation." On another occasion, I remember wanting chocolate and instead praying, "God, please

help Joshua want freedom from this habit more than I want chocolate right now."

Fasting in many ways was guiding my prayers, teaching me how to pray in ways I wouldn't have thought about otherwise. It also deepened my commitment to praying.

Now this type of fasting works only if you choose something that you really enjoy. If I decided to fast from Brussels sprouts or parsnips, it wouldn't do any good, because they aren't a temptation and I will gladly not eat them. It's important to choose something that is important to you.

But it doesn't have to be food.

I have fasted from watching TV, from listening to the radio, from reading anything other than the Bible (I love to read!), and from habits.

Habits?

I have a tendency when I'm doing mindless things, such as cleaning the house, to daydream. It's really silly. I may daydream that Oprah has discovered one of my books, read them all, and is telling the world what a great author I am. Or I may daydream that I've won a home makeover and imagine what all I would do to the house (first thing would be a new kitchen!). But there are times when my daydreams travel from silly, harmless things to daydreaming about situations that are unwise to think about.

So when a young woman from the young-adult class I taught at church stopped attending and moved in with an abusive young man, I chose to fast from daydreaming to pray for her. I began by asking God to remind me to pray for her every time I started to daydream. I continued this fast for about a year and came to the place that I couldn't daydream anymore, even after the fast was over. I'd start to daydream about having a book on the *New York Times* bestseller list, and I'd start to pray instead.

You may not daydream, but may bite your nails, twist your hair, or go raid the fridge.

The key isn't what you're giving up as much as that you're replacing something important in your life with praying for your child about something specific that is very important to you.

## When it's time to stop

How do you know when its time to stop fasting?

When I fasted for the young woman in my class, I stopped when she phoned to tell me she had left the young man and wondered if she'd be welcomed back at church. (Of course she was! It was there that she met her future husband and asked me to be a bridesmaid in her wedding, making me the oldest person in the bridal party.)

When I fasted for Josh, I fasted for more than a year before finally ending the fast. I had not seen the results I was praying for. However, several months later, Josh called and told me that he had given up that particular habit.

I fasted for months for a friend's marriage that was struggling; and despite all the prayers being lifted by me and others, the marriage eventually ended.

As I write this, I am fasting for one week for a possible church plant a lot of us have been talking about seeing started in our community. I chose to put a time limit on this fast, committing to praying and fasting from refined sugars for one week. I've invited others who have a burden for this project to join me. Every time I'm tempted to have something sweet, I'm reminded to pray for this possibility, for God to guide in every detail—to bring together a committed core of leaders, to raise up a godly worship team, to provide the right location, etc.

You may want to choose to fast for one day, one week, one month, or one day a week for a month. You may choose to fast indefinitely.

Make it a matter of prayer between you and God. Ask Him,

"How long?" Commit to praying and fasting for that period of time with Him.

If you choose to fast indefinitely, as I did when praying for Josh to break his habit, keep watch. When you find yourself avoiding whatever you're fasting from out of habit and no longer praying for the specific need, its time to stop. You're no longer truly fasting and praying; the fast has become a habit.

## God's commitment

Fasting does not mean that God will say Yes right then to your prayers. It's not a guarantee for the answer you want, not a surefire way of getting your way.

Fasting is a commitment to something incredibly important to you, a way of showing that commitment, as well as a way to pray more fiercely for something. There are just times as a parent when something is so heavy on your heart that you need and long for a way of praying more fervently for it. There are times, as shown in Matthew 17, when a deeper commitment is needed.

I don't believe that the deeper commitment is needed because we have to convince God to change His mind and answer in a way He wouldn't without our fasting, or that He doesn't really want to give us the strength to break the habit, rescue our kid from a harmful relationship or situation, or give wisdom on an important decision, but our fasting will so impress Him that He'll change His mind and do it. I don't think God is sitting up there oblivious to what our children are wrestling with and needs us to bring it to His attention so that He will do something.

I think fasting is about us.

Every time I've fasted, it has deepened my commitment and my relationship to God. I've learned how to pray in new ways. I've wrestled in prayer over my request, learning to trust God and learning to believe He truly will move

and is moving. I've discovered whether something I'm praying for is truly important to me or not.

Jesus told the disciples that they hadn't healed the child because it took fasting and prayer, and also because of their unbelief. As we choose to fast for those things that break our hearts, we learn to believe more strongly that God does and will answer and that He is at work. Even when my friend's marriage ended despite all the prayers, I still saw God. He transformed my friend. She was always someone pretty special, but through this trial, God grew her deeper and stronger and grew our friendship that way, as well. My heart continues to hurt with her over the loss of her marriage, but I am amazed at what God has done in her life as a result.

As I fast for my children, I am reminded of God's commitment to them. He did more than just give up chocolate or daydreaming for them. He gave His only Son. His heart longs for them more than mine does. And He alone knows the best way to walk them closer toward Him, and He alone is able to redeem the hard things in their lives for good.

## Journal

- Have you ever attempted fasting? If you have, journal about an experience and how God led and what He did in you and through your fast.
- As you've read the chapter, were you impressed about something you would like to commit to prayer and fasting for your children?
- What will you fast from? For how long? When will you begin? Ask God what He wants.
- Write out a prayer committing to God for this fast.

# Praying Like Crazy Together

*"Again I say to you that if two of you agree on earth concerning anything that they ask, it will be done for them by My Father in heaven. For where two or three are gathered together in My name, I am there in the midst of them."*
*—Matthew 18:19, 20*

I enjoy talking about parenting with my friend Linda. Not only because I just appreciate her insights, but because Linda has young-adult sons too. We're both experiencing similar things, such as hairstyles, clothes, heartbreaks, and attitudes, and knowing someone else is in the same place as I am helps it to feel OK—normal—with the assurance that I'm not failing as a parent and that my kids are just being kids their age, and someone else understands this.

Having others join us in our journey of parenting can give us more courage and confidence, whether it's sharing the joys and struggles of parenting in the place and age that we're at or having a parent a little farther along the journey who is able to say, "Oh, that's just a stage. Hang in there. It gets better."

But it is even more strengthening when we come together as parents to pray for our children together. To have someone else listen and then pray for the things on our hearts and to praise and thank God for the joys we're experiencing, can give us that needed courage and confidence as we walk through the different adventures in parenting.

I know that there are others praying for my sons. I so appreciate that! As a mom, it makes me feel loved and cared for to have others love and care for my sons—and to take the time and make the commitment to pray for them.

## Praying with other parents

There are moms who come together to pray for all the children in their local schools. Moms in Touch is a national organization that establishes groups of parents who gather regularly to pray specifically for the school, administrators, teachers, and students in their local public or Christian school. On their Web site, you can check whether there's a group in your area, or find information about how to begin one for your school (www.moms intouch.org).

I've organized a prayer chain called "MUCK—Mothers United in Christ for Our Kids." The women who join commit to praying for the children on the list. They can then submit the names of their children and grandchildren. There aren't specific requests for healing of an illness or finding a job or help with school. This prayer team is praying specifically for the spiritual journeys of each of the children on the team. While they don't pray together, there are mothers across Pennsylvania and beyond praying for approximately three hundred children, young and old.

Yet praying with other parents doesn't have to be an organized ministry. It can be a couple of moms meeting over a hot drink, sharing about their kids, and praying together for their children before they leave. Or dads who take five minutes after the gym to pray for their families. Coworkers at work who do more than just talk about their kids, but spend a few minutes together during lunch lifting each other's children to God. Or friends talking on the phone, realizing that there's a need and praying together right then and there. Recently, I sat in a small café catching up with a friend over cups of tea and was sharing some cool things God was doing in the life of one of my sons. My friend was so excited about what she was hearing that she grabbed my hand and spontaneously began praying and thanking God right there.

Whether it's a weekly or monthly "date," or just a spontaneous prayer at the end of a get-together, praying with other parents not only brings a strength and peace to take with you, but there's power in praying together. God's Word tells us that there's something special about coming together and agreeing in prayer. " 'Again I say to you that if two of you agree on earth concerning anything that they ask, it will be done for them by My Father in heaven. For where two or three are gathered together in My name, I am there in the midst of them' " (Matthew 18:19, 20). God promises to answer. He will answer whether we pray alone or with someone else, but He knows there's something special that happens *for* us when we pray with someone else. We're drawn closer to that person. We feel encouraged. And we've given that gift to another person as well. God wants us to be a body of believers who encourage each other and carry each others' burdens. He challenges us to share our burdens with one another, to encourage one another, and to pray together and for one another. He knows that as we pray together for the things most important to us, it will build the body of believers stronger—closer to Him, closer to each other, and personally encouraged.

We can ask others to pray for our children without sharing every detail of what's happening in their lives.

## Be careful what you say

But a word of caution: as we talk about our kids with other people, we need to be careful what we share and how much we tell. We don't want to betray the confidences our

kids entrust to us. We don't want to share things that would embarrass them. We can ask others to pray for our children without sharing every detail of what's happening in their lives. It's important for children to know that Mom and Dad are people they can talk to and trust that what they tell them isn't told to all of their parents' friends.

It's also important to know that the person you are sharing with will keep your words confidential. We don't want to tell a friend something personal about our children and have them tell someone else, who tells someone else, who tells someone else, who . . . Whisper-down-the-lane usually distorts the original story and typically gets back to the person being talked about.

And as people share prayer needs with us, it's important that we keep them confidential. Sometimes a need seems so great we feel that others should be praying, so we resort to "holy gossip"—sharing private information in the form of a prayer request. Unless we've been told we can tell others and ask them to pray, it's important for us to do the praying and trust God to answer without the help of other prayer warriors.

## Mom and Dad

While it can be a very encouraging and powerful thing to have other parents join you in praying for your children, there is nothing more powerful than a mom and dad who pray for their children together. Really pray, setting aside time to pray specifically for each of their children individually. It is more than a family mealtime prayer, "Lord, please bless Michael and Sara." It is time spent on our knees together with our spouses, praying for our children, for their spouses, and their children.

There's nothing that can unite a couple more powerfully than to pray together, regularly and often, and nothing more important than to pray together for our families.

## Praying Like Crazy Together

Recently our oldest son, Joshua, came home for the holidays. As he was leaving, we asked him if we could pray for him. My husband and I embraced him and took turns praying aloud for him. It felt as if we were standing on holy ground—a sacred moment. While I'm sure it was powerful for Josh to hear his dad pray for him, it also encouraged me to hear my husband pray for our son.

Families are so under attack today. The devil is out to destroy. He wants nothing more than to divide homes—husbands and wives, parents and children. Prayer is one of our greatest tools. It's one way we fight against the attacks. Praying together allows us to stand united as we fight for our children and ask God to move heaven and earth on their behalf.

### Journal

- Remember a time when someone prayed with you, for you and for specific burdens on your heart. Journal about the experience and how it made you feel and how God worked.
- If you're not currently praying with someone and would like to be, pray and ask God who He'd like you to partner with in praying together for your children. It may be someone on the same journey as you, or it may be someone older than you who has already walked down this path.
- When will you approach that person and ask her or him to pray with you?
- Write out a prayer asking God to guide you in praying with another person, when, how, what to pray about, etc.
- What impressed you in this chapter? What would you like to take away and implement in your life as a result?

# Persevering in Prayer

It was one of the toughest experiences of our lives.

Josh's senior year. It had gotten off to a great start. We prayed it would be a good year, fun and challenging. We talked about college and began working on plans for his next step.

Then on an October evening, everything changed.

Josh's friend Ryan died in a car accident. A great year took a devastating twist. Josh and his friends didn't understand why. Nor did we. Things continued to happen. A classmate's leukemia came out of remission. Another classmate was diagnosed with a brain tumor. A close friend's twenty-something brother died while playing soccer. Another classmate was hospitalized with a chronic lung infection. Parents and grandparents died. The school principal told me that he hadn't seen a more difficult year.

Our smiling, happy son couldn't seem to smile anymore. Depression enfolded him. He and his friends made poor choices, picked up habits that concerned us.

## Relentless prayer

I don't think I've ever prayed harder than I did that year. I prayed in the car. I cried to God while cleaning the house. I begged Him to intervene as I prayed through scripture. Praying for Josh and his friends was one of the biggest focuses of my life during that time. It was like unending conversation with God, as I felt helpless to rescue my son, and didn't know what to do except cry out to God.

## When God is silent

I fasted. I prayed. And I asked others to join me.

Yet God appeared silent.

Where was He? Why wasn't He answering? Why weren't things getting better?

I searched my life for sin that might be standing in the way of God's answering.

I looked at the things I was praying for and knew that I was praying according to God's will—I knew God longed for my son to trust Him, to know Him, to walk with Him, and to be healthy physically, mentally, and spiritually.

And still God seemed silent.

My heartache sent me to the book of Job. He knew what it was like to experience devastation and silence. For thirty-seven chapters, Job wrestles, prays, cries, tries to makes sense of it all, is battered by friends, and sits in God's seeming silence. He says, " 'My spirit is broken, / My days are extinguished' " (Job 17:1). He totally experiences God's silence and feels hopeless and broken.

I felt helpless to rescue my son, and didn't know what to do except cry out to God.

Yet Job never gives up. He continues to cry out to God.

Sometimes it is these very moments when we pray and pray and pray, but we continue to feel that God is far away and silent, that we discover what our faith is really made of. Do we really truly believe that God is good and faithful? That He won't leave us or forsake us? That He does hear? That He *is hearing*? That we can trust Him even in the silence?

I really wrestled with God during this time. I wanted Him to answer. I needed Him to rescue my son and make things good again.

I'll admit, there were moments when I considered giving up. Moments when I was tempted to walk away. I even told God that I would walk away if He didn't do something,

because I believed that there was no point praying if God wasn't listening and acting.

But in my heart, I knew He is God. That He is good. That He is trustworthy. And that even in moments of darkness when I couldn't see Him, I could trust His heart. He loves my son and He loves me with a love stronger and fiercer than my love for Josh.

Sometimes it is these very moments when we pray and pray and pray, but continue to feel that God is far away and silent, that we discover what our faith is really made of.

So while I wrestled with God in the dark, I never quit praying.

My prayers were mingled with attempts at praise. "O Lord, I know You love Josh more than I do. So even now when I don't understand, I'm going to choose to trust that You know what You're doing and that You won't let any of this happen for no reason or just to do harm, but You will redeem and rescue. I know that You *are* answering even now."

## God always answers

It's been said that God has three answers: Yes, No, and Wait.

I'd like to challenge that.

During the tough moments when God seemed silent and distant, when I couldn't understand why, I realized something about prayer.

It began with Job.

God speaks up beginning in chapter 38. As I studied and prayed my way through the book of Job, I realized that God never really addresses Job's questions. He doesn't

answer why. He doesn't tell Job why these things happened or what to do with it all. Instead, He reminds Job of who He is, of all He has done.

As I began looking at the way God answered prayers throughout the Bible, I realized that His answer wasn't really, Yes, or No, or even Wait. It was He Himself.

In every case, He responded with a new revelation and understanding of who He is. The answer was always more of Him.

When He didn't come and heal Lazarus, but chose to wait and then raise him from the dead, Mary and Martha experienced God in a way they never had before. They knew He was a God who could heal. But they didn't know Him as a God who could do the impossible, who could show up when all hope was gone and bring hope like they had never known before. (They believed that the spirit lingered near the body for three days, so there was hope of resurrection for three days. Jesus showed up on day four.)

When Jesus asked the man by the pool, "Do you want to be healed?" the man responded only with excuses of why healing wasn't possible. And Jesus showed him that the impossible was possible.

Looking at the way God answered prayers throughout the Bible, I realized that His answer wasn't really, Yes, or No, or even Wait. It was He Himself.

When Paul prayed three times for healing, but God said No, Paul learned of God's strength to enable him to live with the thorn. He really didn't get a No as much as he got more of God.

When God was silent and didn't immediately bring Josh's smile back, but allowed it to take months and months and months, I learned that I could depend on God, that I could be real and honest about how I felt, and that He would truly still be right there with me.

## It isn't easy

It isn't easy persevering in prayer when you want answers now.

It can be hard trusting a God who appears to be silent, especially when you know He could just speak the word, and it would be done.

One of the hardest things in the world is watching your child hurt or watching your child walk without God day after day, praying and longing for God to move mountains, but going days, weeks, months, even years without the hoped-for answer.

Yet He calls us to continue to pray and trust, to continue to stand on His promises, to experience a deeper dependence on Him, and to believe anyway that He is answering and that He does care.

I still don't understand that dark year in Josh's life. But I've given up my need to know why and am just trusting God. Slowly, Josh learned to smile again. Life has never gone back to the way it was before the accident. And I still struggle with some of the changes. But both Josh and I learned that God never lets go—and neither should we.

## Journal

- Have you ever felt like giving up in prayer, as if praying wasn't accomplishing anything? Or that God was just silent? Journal about that time. What did you do? Give that time to God. If you still feel that He never responded, give that to Him. Confess to Him the hurt you feel. Ask Him to forgive you of the doubt that stirred in your heart.
- Remember a time when you relentlessly persevered in prayer. Journal about the time. What did you experience? Feel? How did God respond? Write a prayer of thanks to God for carrying you through that time.

## Persevering in Prayer

- Have there been times when God has answered your prayers with more of Him—more understanding of who He is? Or perhaps He revealed Himself in ways that you really hadn't understood Him before? Write about an experience and what you learned.
- About what are you currently persevering in prayer?
- Write a prayer telling God that you will pray relentlessly and thank Him that He is working and is faithful.
- What impressed you in this chapter? Was there anything that you will take away that has encouraged you in your journey?

# God *Is* Answering

I've met parents across the country who have prayed for their children for years. Some for years and years. They pray. They wait. And wait. They continue to persevere in prayer.

I've experienced it myself. Praying and praying. Waiting and waiting. Learning to trust even when it appears God is silent.

## God isn't really silent

But I've learned that God isn't really silent. He's not just sitting in heaven, listening to our prayers, and not responding. He's not waiting for us to ask often enough, or in the right words. He's not waiting for us to do enough for Him first, or waiting for us to offer Him the right thing in exchange. We don't have to somehow convince God.

He *is* answering. He is working, moving on the hearts of our children, nudging them, and convicting them. The work that's going on is "inside" work. He's speaking to their hearts and minds. It's work that we may not see happening. They may not talk about it. But God is working. And He knows what it will take to answer our prayers, to draw our children closer, to reach our prodigals, and to teach them the lessons they need to learn in order to be the people He created them to be. He knows the experiences they need to walk through to find their way to Him, or even just what they need to experience so they learn to share, or have the courage to walk into that first-grade class, or to make a new friend.

## Thank Him even if you can't see

We may not always see what God is doing, but He is

working and responding to our prayers. Sometimes it is easy to forget that God loves our kids and wants even more for them than we do. Sometimes because we don't see anything happening—or what we want to see happening—we can feel as if we have to try harder to convince God because He's not doing anything. Our life experiences can color what we believe about God.

One way to help us remember that He is a loving God who cares about our children and wants their best is to praise Him and thank Him for these very things. (We'll talk more about praise and thanksgiving in our next chapter.) Another way is to thank Him for what He is doing, even if we can't see it. Instead of going to Him and pleading and begging and trying to word our prayer in a different way or convince God to move, ask and then thank Him for what He is doing. "Thank You, Lord, for the way You are working in Jill's life. I don't see anything happening, but I am trusting that You know what's best and are working. Thank You for doing what's necessary in her life."

By thanking Him for what He is doing, even though we can't see it, we are reminded that He is working.

By thanking Him for what He is doing, even though we can't see it, we are reminded that He is working. As we talk and act as if God is working, it will help to convince us that He is, giving us more peace and confidence, building our trust and our expectation.

## Keep looking

Often God gives us glimpses that He's working. We may miss them because we're watching so intently for the end result. As we believe that God is working, we may begin expecting to see glimpses of Him at work. This awareness

and expectation may open our eyes to the little steps God is taking in our children's life to answer our prayers.

Seeing the little steps always gives me courage.

I had been praying for one of my sons and a relationship he was in. One day we were just sitting and talking, and he began sharing things with me that showed that God was at work. He was answering my prayers. I wasn't "seeing" any big changes in my son, but as he shared from his heart, I could see that God had been doing a work all along. Some difficult situations had happened that had been instrumental in the changes taking place in his thinking and heart.

I see these "glimpses" of God at work often when I'm really listening and believing. They come in quiet moments, conversations, and in watching.

## Peace is contagious

When parents begin living with the belief that God is at work, that we don't need to talk Him into answering our prayers or moving on behalf of our prayers, we will live with peace and with confidence that He who began a good work will be faithful to complete it.

Such peace is contagious. It spreads to other parents as we talk with and encourage them.

I see . . . "glimpses" of God at work often when I'm really listening and believing. They come in quiet moments.

But it also spreads to our kids.

A friend of mine went through a bit of a rebellious time as a young person. It drove her mom crazy. She not only prayed for her daughter, but ranted and raved a bit to her. Whenever they were on the phone or visiting, she would remind her young-adult child of how she should be living. She'd cry. She'd beg. It did nothing to draw my friend back or want to talk to her mom often.

Then one day, the ranting and raving and crying and all of it disappeared. It was replaced by a phone call with no reminder of what God would want, or begging her to change her ways. After a few phone calls with nothing but conversations and "I love you," my friend was curious. What had happened to her mom? What had made the change?

> He may work more slowly than you or I would like, but He knows the best way to do it. . . . He wants to take our children deeper. He wants to reach their hearts and make it real.

She asked. Her mom told her that she knew that God would do a work in her daughter's life and that she didn't need to be afraid or rant and rave or convince her daughter. God would.

That belief and peace strongly influenced my friend's life. Today she serves God through an incredibly passionate and inspiring life. She's influenced many young people herself. And it began with a mom who found peace in believing that God was at work and would complete the work.

## Just trusting

I know that God is at work in the lives of my sons. I pray like crazy every day, but I also trust Him. I remind myself that God loves them more than I do and that He is at work and won't let them go without a fight.

I've reminded them of that. I've reminded them that God is going to do big things in their lives—even in the moments of their lives when they haven't been fully living for Him.

I've also reminded them that He will lead.

Recently, Josh came home for a visit and shared some of

his current journey with God. He talked about some of the things he doesn't understand, some of the things that cause him to question and wonder. We've talked. I've shared what I believe and pointed him to Scripture and books that I think will help answer his questions. I've encouraged him in his seeking. I've promised him that God will be found as he seeks and that God *wants* him to really know Him.

I haven't tried to convince Josh or defend God. I know God is big enough to defend Himself and show who He really is to Josh. I see the seeking as God answering my prayers, taking Josh deeper and making his relationship with God real and personal.

God is at work.

He may work more slowly than you or I would like, but He knows the best way to do it. He never wants just a surface answer. He wants to take our children deeper. He wants to reach their hearts and make it real.

## Journal

- Remember ways that God has answered your prayers. Journal a few experiences of answered prayers and thank God for what He's done.
- What are some of the things that you are currently praying for but aren't seeing God answering? Make a list.
- Write out a prayer thanking God for what He is doing in each of these requests, even if you can't see anything. Thank Him for knowing the best way to work in your children so that their relationship goes deep. Ask Him to deepen your trust and to open your eyes to the ways that the Holy Spirit is moving.
- What in this chapter impressed you as you read? What will you take away?

# Praise and Thanksgiving

We're thinking a lot about thanksgiving this week. As I write this, Americans are preparing for Thanksgiving, the holiday, a time when families gather to eat a big meal, watch a few parades and some football, and think about the things they're thankful for.

Admittedly, most may think only about the meal and the football. It's easy for us to forget what the day was designed to be about—giving thanks. We may even lose sight of the things for which we can be thankful when there are so many things we still want and so many struggles we're facing.

Prayer is the same way.

It's easy to get so caught up in the asking, seeking, and knocking that we forget to give thanks. Yet the Bible tells us that thanksgiving needs to be a part of our prayer life.

"Rejoice always, pray without ceasing, in everything give thanks; for this is the will of God in Christ Jesus for you" (1 Thessalonians 5:16–18).

"Be anxious for nothing, but in everything by prayer and supplication, with thanksgiving, let your requests be made known to God; and the peace of God, which surpasses all understanding, will guard your hearts and minds through Christ Jesus" (Philippians 4:6, 7).

"Let us come before His presence with thanksgiving" (Psalm 95:2).

"Enter into His gates with thanksgiving, / And into His courts with praise. / Be thankful to Him, and bless His name" (Psalm 100:4).

## Being thankful

Being thankful is a tricky thing.

When things are going well, it's easy to take it for granted and forget to give thanks.

When things are tough, it's easy to be so caught up in the difficult and praying for the needs that we forget to be thankful or can't think of anything to be thankful for.

Yet the Bible is pretty clear that we need to be thankful in everything. Good or bad. The psalmist challenges us to "enter His gates" and "come before His presence" with thanksgiving. I've taken that up as a discipline to begin my prayer time with thanks. Not every prayer. Those prayers I send up throughout the day are short and sweet, but when I sit down with God and journal out my prayers, I begin with thanksgiving. I think over the previous day, or that day if I'm journaling in the evening, and try to look for everything for which I can think of to be thankful.

> It's often in the hard things that we learn the most. So I'm learning to trust God with the struggles and battles and thank Him for being faithful.

Some are big things. This morning I was thanking God that Josh is coming home for the holidays. It's been a few months since I've gotten to hang out with him, and I can't wait! Sometimes it's something simple, such as a good conversation, a good attitude, or a glimpse that he's learning responsibility.

I look for ways God is working in our sons' lives. I thank Him for growth that I see happening, for important things, such as new jobs and opportunities, or the car finally getting fixed. I watch for God answering my prayers on their behalf and thank Him.

## The hard stuff

I've even learned to thank God for the hard lessons. I wish He could just zap my kids, and they'd be mature and deeply spiritual and passionate and have purpose and amazing relationships with friends and a godly woman. But life is typically hard. Yet it's often in the hard things that we learn the most. So I'm learning to trust God with the struggles and battles and thank Him for being faithful in teaching my sons and growing them into the men He's created them to be.

Admittedly, there are some things I just don't understand. Battles and struggles they've faced that I don't understand. Things that I wish they hadn't had to go through, such as Ryan's death and broken hearts. Yet I can still thank God that while my view and understanding is limited, His isn't. He knows the reason. He knows the good He's going to bring or even has brought and I haven't seen yet.

## Praising Him

It's especially in the difficult times that I transition from thanksgiving to praise. Praising Him for being a God who knows what's best, wants the eternal best, and is working it all together; praising Him for being trustworthy even when I don't understand what He's doing. Praise reminds me that God is bigger than any problem or challenge we face. It gives me the courage to live the saying, "Don't tell God how big the storm is; tell the storm how big your God is."

Praise focuses on God, on His character, on who He is, and on what He's about.

When I'm praying for my children and I begin to praise God, I'm reminded of all He is for them. He is their Provider. He is their Protector. He is merciful to them, pouring out blessings and grace. He is their Defender. He is their Healer. He is the Shepherd who will lay everything else aside to go looking for them.

Most important for me, praise always reminds me that God loves Josh and Zach more than I do or possibly could, that not only does He want what's best for them, but He knows what's best and can lead them to what's best.

## It's all about Him

Praise and thanksgiving take the focus off of our children and places it on God. It reminds us that He is working on their behalf and will continue to do so. It encourages us that He is trustworthy and merciful. It gives us the strength and courage to keep praying and believing.

## Journal

- Look over your parenting journey. Make a list of things that you are thankful for, both big things and little things. Write out a prayer to God for these things.
- How easy is it to give thanks for the hard things? What hard things are your children currently experiencing for which you haven't given thanks? Write out a prayer and thank God for what He will do through the hard things. Ask Him to help you see how to be thankful.
- Thanksgiving and praise are two different things. Thanksgiving is thanking God for what He's done. Praise is responding to who He is. What are things for which you would like to praise God? Make a list of God's characteristics that you appreciate.
- Many scripture passages are filled with praise and thanksgiving. The book of Psalms contains many praise and thanksgiving prayers. Claim and make a few scripture passages your own. Write them out as prayers. Here are a few to get you started: Psalm 100 (read through and claim the verses that resonate in your heart); Psalm 103; Psalm 107; Psalm 111.

# The Power of Praying

It was a tough time in my life. I was weary from the battles. Parenting was hard. I had gone to God for hope. I felt impressed to turn to Jeremiah 31. " 'Yes, I have loved you with an everlasting love; / Therefore with lovingkindness I have drawn you' " (verse 3), kept running through my mind. I believed God wanted to remind me of His love for me.

So I opened my Bible and began reading from the beginning of the chapter:

> "The people who survived the sword
> Found grace in the wilderness—
> Israel, when I went to give him rest" (verse 2).

In the margin of my Bible, I began writing a prayer, "Lord, my spirit and heart are so weary. I feel like I'm in a wilderness with parenting."

I began reading through the entire passage, praying the verses back to God, crying out to God for my kids. As God spoke of what He would do for His children, I asked Him to do these very things for my children. "O Lord, save Josh and Zach [verse 7], gather them to You [verse 8], lead them and keep them from stumbling [verse 9]. You have redeemed Josh and Zach [verse 11]. Please, Father! Let us feel well watered and sorrow no more. My heart is so broken [verse 12]. Cause us to rejoice [verse 13], fill our souls, let my sons be satisfied with You alone and look nowhere else for what they need [verse 14]."

God stopped me in my tracks when I got to verses 16 and 17:

## Praying Like Crazy for Your Kids

> "Refrain your voice from weeping
> And your eyes from tears;
> For your work shall be rewarded, says the LORD,
> And they shall come back from the land of the enemy.
> There is hope in your future, says the LORD,
> That your children shall come back to their own border."

I had come to God in tears. I had cried out to Him, asking Him, Why? After I had sacrificed so much for my sons! Why didn't it look like I wanted it to? I thought that if I did all the "right" things that my sons would grow up to be godly, passionate men who served God in everything. I made my list to God of all I had done. I had prayed. I had quit my career to stay home and be with them. I had read books to them. I had played with them. I had disciplined them. I had taken them to church and Sabbath School. I had taught them to be involved. We had even changed our church membership, driving twice as far as we had been, leaving the only church I had ever been a member of and where my husband attended since he was a kid, so that our sons could be in a church with an active youth group. Even after going back to work, I made sure I accepted only jobs that allowed me to work while the boys were in school, so that I could be home when they were home. We had paid for Christian education from kindergarten through high school. We had scrimped on everything to make ends meet. We drove them back and forth every day for years. I angrily and brokenheartedly turned to God, "Why, Lord? Why didn't it end up the way I wanted? Why didn't my efforts pay off?"

> As God spoke of what He would do for His children, I asked Him to do these very things for my children.

Very gently God spoke to me. Very specifically.

He reminded me that He loved me and He sent me to a verse that reminded me of that and so much more.

He nudged me to pray for my sons as I read through all He had promised His children.

And then He landed me on this verse.

How like God!

Stop crying. "Your work will be rewarded." God knew all the sacrifices I had made. He had made even greater ones. He knew my efforts would make a difference. He would be the One to reward my effort.

> I angrily and brokenheartedly turned to God, "Why, Lord? Why didn't it end up the way I wanted? Why didn't my efforts pay off?"

"Your kids will come home."

As I've traveled across the country and even into Australia, speaking at women's retreats and camp meetings, I've encountered parent after parent whose heart is breaking for their children, wondering if they'll ever come home. It's one of the biggest burdens I see mothers carrying. They long for their children and grandchildren to walk intimately with God. Their hearts break when they don't. It doesn't seem to matter who they are. I've listened to moms who weren't walking with God when they raised their children and now are and longing for their children to catch the joy they've found. I've sat with mothers who are leaders in their churches and have worked for their denomination, leading others to Christ, but having their children reject Him.

They wonder, *Do my prayers and efforts make any difference?*

God says, "Yes. Your work will be rewarded."

Our children still have freedom of choice, but God will do all, using all the resources of heaven, to pursue our children and bring their hearts home—whether they've

wandered far or perhaps are even in church, but just not passionate and are instead just living a life of habit—go to church, live your life; two separate things.

We want so much for them!

So we pray. And God says it makes a difference. There is power in the prayers of parents and grandparents. Our prayers are heard and do make a difference.

I was reading through a book with advice and guidelines for parents and came across a quote written in the 1800s by a woman named Ellen White. The language is a little different from how we speak today, but the message is powerful:

> It is impossible to estimate the power of a praying mother's influence. She acknowledges God in all her ways. She takes her children before the throne of grace and presents them to Jesus, pleading for His blessing upon them. The influence of those prayers is to those children as a "wellspring of life." These prayers, offered in faith, are the support and strength of the Christian mother. To neglect the duty of praying with our children is to lose one of the greatest blessings within our reach, one of the greatest helps amid the perplexities, cares, and burdens of our lifework.
>
> The power of a mother's prayers cannot be too highly estimated. She who kneels beside her son and daughter through the vicissitudes of childhood, through the perils of youth, will never know till the judgment the influence of her prayers upon the life of her children. If she is connected by faith with the Son of God, the mother's tender hand may hold back her son from the power of temptation, may restrain her daughter from indulging in sin. When passion is warring for the mastery, the power of love, the restraining, earnest, determined influence

of the mother, may balance the soul on the side of right.[1]

Our prayers make a difference. Without them, we lose one of the greatest sources of strength and help we can have as a parent. We may never know until heaven the difference they have made in the lives of our children, the battles won on our knees, the temptations and evil held back, the protection our kids enjoyed, and the blessings given to them because we intentionally prayed like crazy.

One day, God may set us down in heaven and pull up His "home movies" for us to watch. He'll show us the behind-the-scenes footage that we can't see now: the power our prayers gave angels as they protected and guided our children; the times our prayers empowered the Holy Spirit to speak to and convict our children of right and wrong; and the moments the devil was forced back because we stood in the gap with our prayers.

Then we'll know. Praying like crazy for our kids was one of the most powerful things we did as parents.

## Journal

- How have you seen the power of prayer in the lives of your children as you've prayed? Write about those experiences. Give God thanks and praise.
- What do you believe about the power of prayer? Do you believe that *your* prayers truly make a difference in the lives of your children?
- If you do, write a prayer thanking God for the power of prayer and for how He's using your prayers for your children.
- If you doubt, tell God honestly what you feel and think.

## Praying Like Crazy for Your Kids

Like the father who cried out, "I believe, help my unbelief," ask God to strengthen your belief and to encourage and strengthen your belief in Him and prayer.

- What has encouraged you the most in this chapter? What will you take away?
- Claim and pray scripture passages that promise that God hears and answers our prayers: Matthew 7:7; 21:22; John 11:22; 14:12–14; Hebrews 4:16.
- What other scripture passages would you like to claim as you trust God to answer prayers?

---

1. Ellen G. White, *The Adventist Home* (Hagerstown, Md.: Review and Herald® Publishing Association, 1952, 1980), 266.

### Additional Resources

Blaine Bartel, *7 Absolutes to Pray Over Your Kids* (Tulsa, Okla.: Harrison House, 2005).

Stormie Omartian, *The Power of a Praying Parent* (Eugene, Ore.: Harvest House, 1995).